BABIES
CELEBRATED

BÉATRICE FONTANEL • CLAIRE D'HARCOURT

BABIES CELEBRATED

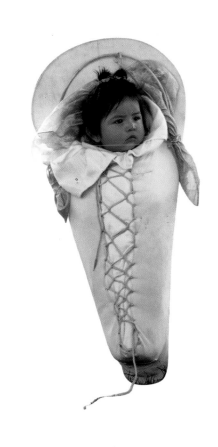

Harry N. Abrams, Inc., Publishers

To our parents
Lucette and Georges Fontanel
and Jeanne-Marie and Arnoult d'Harcourt

Acknowledgments

We thank all of the researchers, conservationists, and documentarians who helped us, in particular Alain Epelboin and Annie Marx who opened the doors of their medical laboratory to us; Marie Geysen for her careful translations; and Maguette Dumont of the picture library of the Musée de L'Homme. We are also grateful to all of the others who have assisted us: Françoise Aubaille; Néna Baratier; Réjane Batard-Boyer, CNRS; Serge Bahuchet, CNRS audiovisual; Emmanuelle Carbonnier; Marie-France Casevitz, CNRS; Dominique Champault; Françoise Cousin, CNRS; Pascale Dollfus, Musée de L'Homme; Marguerite Dupire; Maryvonne Fortier and Marie-Christine Chedel; Monique Galland-Dravet, CIDEF; Christiane Grin, CNRS audiovisual; Roberte Hamayon, Ethnology Laboratory, Paris X; Christine Hemmet, E.P.H.E., CNRS; Gisèle Krauskopff, Musée de L'Homme; Jean-Luc Lambert; Nicole de Larocque Latour; Arlette Liebert, Sushila Manandhar, CNRS; Catherine Mangeot; Josiane Massard-Vincent, Center for Nepal and Asian Studies, Kathmandu; Geneviève Najar, CNRS; Anne-Marie Patrick, CNRS; Bernadette Robbe, Laboratory of Comparative Ethnology and Sociology, Paris X; and Emmanuel Valentin, Musée de L'Homme.

Opposite:
Clockwise:
Baby carriers from Borneo, New Guinea, and Senegal.

Preceding page:
Sudan.
A Dinka mother with her child.

Editor, English-language edition: Ellen Nidy
Design Coordinator, English-language edition: Dana Sloan
Art Director, Paul-Raymond Cohen

Library of Congress Cataloguing-in-Publication Data
Fontanel, Béatrice.
    [Bébé du monde. English]
    Babies Celebrated / by Béatrice Fontanel and Claire d'Harcourt ;
        translated from the French by Jack Hawkes.
        p.   cm.
    ISBN 0-8109-4012-4
    1. Infants—Folklore—Cross-cultural studies. 2. Infants—Care—
    Cross-cultural studies. 3. Birth customs—Cross-cultural studies.
    I. D'Harcourt, Claire, 1960- . II. Title.
    GR475.F6313 1998
    392. 1'3—dc21   98-24593

Printed and bound in Italy

Harry N. Abrams, Inc.
100 Fifth Avenue
New York, N.Y. 10011
www.abramsbooks.com

Contents

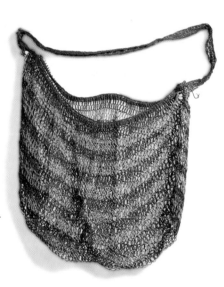

Preface

Why a Book on Tribal Babies?

The study of the baby is significant for anyone who is interested in early childhood, or anyone who studies practices of other times or places relating to early childhood. An infant instantly captures our sympathy and empathy. When we are presented with the photograph of a baby, even one that looks foreign to us, cultural distance vanishes. At first glance, every infant's way of life seems based on the satisfaction of the same elementary needs, such as eating and elimination, and therefore appears easy enough to decipher. But then we discover the extent to which child-rearing practices differ in other cultures; for example, some societies manipulate the baby's body materially as well as symbolically. As Western parents discover these "exotic" child-care techniques, they say to themselves, "Aha! Of course, other people do things differently than we do." Of the array of child-rearing techniques from around the world, some resonate with us more than others—we then adopt them ourselves, thereby practicing a form of "neo-massage" or "neo-carrying."

As we learn more about the child-rearing techniques of other societies, our curiosity increases, reinforcing our need to learn more. Sometimes we are deliciously shocked to hear, for example, how an African mother may clean her baby's nose by sucking out the mucus (which she then spits out); at the same time, however, studying the children of others invites us to reexamine the nature of our relationships with our own children. Exploring how early childhood is treated in other cultures is useful because it necessitates a revision of our own practices and theories.

I became interested in early childhood for a quite trivial reason. As an ethnologist doing field research, I am bored most of the time. Nothing happens. In the societies I am studying, time is imprecise; it stretches out and breaks down. To distract myself, I look around. What crystallizes the attention, the rhythms, and the mood of a community? The baby. In these civilizations—as in our own—the baby is a tyrant-king. After spending an entire day with a baby, I realized that I saw an entire society stream by: parents, uncles and aunts, brothers and sisters, and neighbors. The baby is like a thread in a tangled skein: one pull and the entire society is unraveled. In addition to giving us pleasure, the baby is an incredibly fascinating anthropological subject.

Alain Epelboin, Doctor and Ethnologist at the
National Center for Scientific Research, France

China.
A Mongol father
and his child in the
Qinghai region.

7

Introduction

It may seem revolting to use dung for a baby's diaper, until we realize that it is the clever practice of herdsmen who know how to utilize everything their flocks provide, even the waste. It may seem crazy to offer water at a crossroads in order to keep a baby from crying, until we realize that it is the manifestation of a complicated system of beliefs—a system that is much more complex than the organized religion found in modern urban societies. To make rash assumptions about dung diapers, or about the practice of offering water at a crossroads—which symbolizes sending the tears of a baby back to the place from which they came—is to reject these practices without understanding their coherent complexity in both the material world and in the realm of religious symbolism. To disregard these practices is to underestimate the intellectual and creative dynamism of a society that inscribes each of its elements within a cultural totality; it is to risk distorting the sense of these elements that exist as parts of a rational whole.

Universality?

All parents are confronted with the same problems: how best to ensure the survival of their children; how to keep them clean; how to stop them from crying; and how to protect them from the invisible world—whether bacterial or spiritual—that threatens them.

To this range of questions there is a multitude of answers. Each specific solution selected by a given society can be understood only within the context of the culture that produced it. Whether the solutions involve using diapers of dung or cotton, or involve the practice of mothers hanging their baby between their legs, or using dogs to gobble up babies' feces, they are all valid solutions to the initial problem of separating a child from his or her waste. These solutions reflect the ingenuity of any given society; an ingenuity that may have no correlation to the level of technology

Zaire.
A Mangbetu mother with her child, whose skull has been shaped with twisted liana.

Vanuatu.
A baby whose skull is
compressed in a hat.

attained by that society. Each of these child-care techniques reveals a
degree of efficacy. However comical or shocking they may seem to us,
these means of disposing of the baby's excrement represent the attempts
of various cultures to resolve a universal problem. Child-care solutions
are numerous, but they may all be grouped together under a few cate-
gories defined by their common approach.

These solutions—which range from inserting a little tube into the
baby's pants to quickly interpreting the wriggling of a baby who is being
carried—remind us that every culture is an invention modulated by the
culture's history and the constraints of the environment. However, they
all reflect a human spirit and a sense of humor with regard to the body.

Why Compare?

For quite some time, ethnologists and psychologists have been eager to collect and compare the variety of methods by which parents rear and educate their offspring. Are the parents strict or indulgent? Are they concerned foremost with educating their babies or with allowing them instant gratification? From this perspective, it is clear that the chief concern of pediatricians in the West during the first half of the twentieth century was not the needs of the child, but rather how quickly the child developed.

On the other hand, different societies have different objectives: Nomadic Pygmies value the group's solidarity above all else, and turn every woman into a relay-mother. West African peoples place a premium on sharing, and teach this to children early on by giving them objects and food that must be shared or relinquished, thereby teaching them the common nature of goods, the necessity of distributing them equally, and the importance of being able to give them up temporarily.

Environment, technology, and social and ethical ideas are the factors that shape the child-rearing techniques of different peoples. It is misleading to think that the only difference between nonindustrial and industrial countries is a "natural" style of child rearing in developing countries versus an "artificial" style in Western countries; or to think

Tanzania.
Babies carried in goat skins decorated with beads, cowrie shells, bottle caps, buttons, and pierced coins.

that child care in far-off countries has an archaic simplicity that is in contrast with the complexity of Western child-care institutions. If we believe that child-care in nonindustrial countries is more tender and nurturing, we must also note that these same societies employ child-rearing practices that are sophisticated, directive, and that aim to improve the baby's body (through massage), and impart to the baby an inner-strength and dignity (through the customs of dressing or carrying). Good parents with exacting practices do not come exclusively, or even predominately, from the West.

Washing

Cultural ideas about indulgence and strictness are particularly well illustrated by the manner in which women around the world wash their babies. The bath can be an important time for sharing and expressing tenderness, a welcome time for relaxation, and a time when the mother can teach her child how to communicate. In other cultures, however, baths are a time when babies are vigorously scrubbed, their orifices assaulted, and their eyes made to burn from the soap.

Body to Body or at a Distance?

In the West during the early twentieth century, between the use of soap, washcloths, towels, and cradles, mothers touched their babies relatively little. This differs greatly from bathing practices in the tropics, where the soaping and rinsing of the baby are performed on the mother's legs or in the lap of the parent, grandparent, or midwife. However, today in the West, tactile relations between the mother and child are now finally encouraged as a guarantor of healthy development.

Sensory Communication

In industrial societies, mothers are encouraged to focus their children's attention. They talk to their babies as they bathe them, play games with them, and look into their eyes: in short, mothers do everything possible to obtain a response from their babies. Western parents believe babies develop more quickly this way. But some peoples do not share this

Uganda.
A mother carrying her child, who is protected by a calabash.

opinion. Some mothers set about washing their babies in silence in the belief that babies are not yet sufficiently attached to the world of the living. Others, in the belief that an infant is born already understanding earthly discourse, talk to the child in the language of an adult. Some peoples believe that direct exchange with a baby is a waste of time; the mother does not talk to or look at the baby she is bathing. However, while bathing her baby, the mother is simultaneously developing rich relationships with other adults and older children all around. Although indirect, the scope and diversity of these exchanges are instructive for the baby.

Burkina Faso.
A mother with her baby, whose head is protected by a calabash.

Exercise and Massage

Zaire.
A Logo woman carrying her child in a wooden baby carrier.

In contrast with the relative rapidity with which babies in the West are washed and dressed, babies in the Near East and Africa are handled a great deal during the bathing process. In India, among the upper classes, massages gently and harmoniously extend the baby's bath. In Africa, the practice of massage is also found, with important variations ranging from meticulous pressure on specific joints to vigorous kneading of the entire body.

In many places in the world, the newborn is the object of an often spectacular manipulation that might best be described as physical education. Experts in childhood development believe that these physical practices teach children early in life a sense of their physical limits, as well as their dynamic possibilities, and that these babies therefore enjoy an advantage over other babies with less physical training.

Infusions and Washing

In some parts of the world, baths are associated with washings, potions, and enemas using water in which various plants have been steeped or boiled. These practices usually take place in a therapeutic setting for the adult; the traditional healer treats his or her patients with infusions and herb teas that are simultaneously applied externally (in the form of an ablution) and internally (in the form of a drink). In

Africa, these treatments are administered to babies for their tonic
virtues and to prevent illness.

By looking at these ancient methods of child rearing, we see that
societies with the reputation of being traditional are in fact more active
and directive with regard to their infants than industrial societies are,
even though the latter are reputed to be in constant search of improve-
ment and innovation.

Clothing and Ornamentation

Clothes are a significant indication of the joining of the child with his or
her culture, as well as an important marker of sex, age, and the socio-
economic level of the family to which he or she belongs.

Let us begin with the custom of swaddling. This manner of dressing
infants was practiced in ancient Greece and Roman Gaul, and is today

practiced in China, Yemen, South America, and among the Bataks of Sumatra. Historians have been able to duplicate various historical styles of swaddling, from crossed ribbons holding a single piece of cloth wrapping in place, like on bas-reliefs, to a spiral-wound cloth, like in Italian miniatures from the Middle Ages, to large squares of cloth that are braided together. There are reasons for the persistence of this custom: swaddling not only guarantees warmth during a cold winter, it satisfies the parent's desire for a firm baby by binding together the baby's limbs, thus creating an artificial but reassuring solidity.

Swaddling also molds the baby by the very immobility to which it condemns him or her. An indication of the authoritative attitude of adults toward children, swaddling is the reverse image of massage. When practiced for a long period, swaddling has containing and even coercive powers with regard to the movement it prevents. Swaddling infants is a way to assuage parental anxiety over the infant's vulnerability, but it also represents the parent's desire to thwart the infant's movements, which mark the beginnings of his or her autonomy.

Indicators of Sex, Status, and Social Class

Clothing and ornamention serve as "markers"—a way to make visible or reinforce those differences that are judged to be socially significant. Today in West Africa, girls' ears are pierced in the first few days following

Brazil.
A mother carrying her sick child in a woven sash.

birth. In this way, girls are distinguished from boys even when they are wrapped up in their mother's scarf, which covers everything but the baby's head. Throughout the last century in Europe, on the other hand, both male and female toddlers wore dresses so that even by the age of two, visually, nothing distinguished boys from girls.

Even more important than marking gender, clothing illustrates the child's social status. In Asia and the Near East, the quality of the material and the choice and value of the jewelry indicate the political power or the economic weight of the child's relatives. Children's clothing reveals the social disparities in a society.

Unfortunately, many of the exotic ornaments and the extremely rich apparel pictured in this book are nothing more than photographic memories. The excesses of splendor have given way to the relative uniformity of clothing inspired by Western fashion.

Brazil.
A Kayapo mother
with her child.

Carrying the Baby

In charting the range of physical closeness between adults and children, we may conclude that direct contact with the parent gives the child a greater sense of security and happiness, while also proving more agreeable for the adult. In various temperate climates, body-to-body contact between the parent and child is weakened because adults wear heavy clothing and use strollers or animals to carry children, rather than carrying them naked on their back. The nature of the climate alone doesn't explain everything: while it is true that in Mali or the Congo, the baby is carried wrapped in a scarf, in the Arctic, Inuit babies are carried naked in the hoods of the parent's anorak. The culture, rather than the climate, determines the degree of physical closeness that is morally acceptable, depending on the child's age and his or her relation to the adult.

Vertical Posture versus Horizontal

In a stroller, the recumbent baby does not perceive a great deal of the surrounding world. Carried on parents' backs, however, the baby is subject to much richer and more frequent visual and auditory stimuli.

Being carried on the mother's back introduces the baby gradually to various activities: babies are tossed about on nights of dancing, add their weight to the search for water, and bend to the earth when the mother is weeding a field. In many rural societies, parents continue to carry their infants while engaged in activities related to subsistence, domestic chores, or the exercise of a trade. When the baby is as one with the mother's body, he or she serves as a witness to all this work.

Putting the Baby to Bed

The theme of the cradle brings up the issue of parental strictness versus indulgence. This is shown in the famous aphorism: "The best cradle is one that doesn't rock." At the beginning of the century, doctors in the West believed that this practice, and others, made parents "slaves" to their own children. However, with the important exception of peoples who sleep on mats or who share beds that rock with their children, rocking babies in cradles seems to have a universal appeal.

Lami men and women, a fishing people who live on an island in the China Sea, build a system of oars around the beds of their children and then rock the bed like a small boat on the sea. These horizontal rocking impulses echo the vertical rocking practice of peasants in Sumatra who attach a pulley to a piece of cloth rolled around the baby, creating an up-and-down rocking movement.

Lullabies are also universal. From the Pygmies of the Central African Republic to the islanders of Oceania, from the Mossi of Burkina Faso, who describe in hushed tones the entire family tree, to the Albanians whose songs have political overtones, people around the world sing to their babies. While falling asleep, children are given access to a wider universe. In industrial societies, cradles and lullabies are thought to be old-fashioned ways of calming children and helping them fall asleep. However, as pediatricians in industrial countries become more vocal in their opposition to the practice of giving sedatives to babies, these traditional practices may enjoy a justified return to favor.

New Caledonia.
A "shelf" baby carrier.

Oman.
A cradle carried with a forehead strap.

Afghanistan.
A cradle hammock.

Superstition or Religion?

Many approaches to child-raising problems do not fall under the rubric of what would be considered practical solutions in the West. In matters of children's survival, and in issues regarding children's health and development, solutions of magical or religious nature greatly outnumber material solutions. Indeed, in the eyes of many peoples, if the latter prove successful, it is only because the former have not been neglected.

Aesthetics or Supernatural Protection?

It is important to understand the ornamentation of babies for what it really is. In Africa, the amulets worn by almost-naked young children are not there for decoration; they give protection against specific illnesses, or help the child acquire various physical benefits. In India, the baby's makeup helps bring him or her closer to the revered Buddha; in Afghanistan, the color of the stone in the bracelet worn by a child gives protection against the "evil eye."

Invisible Protection and Danger

It is difficult to separate the child-care approaches that fall under the category of religion from those that fall under the category of superstition. The approach belongs to the latter when the objective of the parents is

18

Algeria.

A young woman
with a swaddled
baby.

Syria.
A mother holding her child.

Greenland.
A mother carrying
her baby in her hood.

to "short-circuit" the religious process, and when the ritual is not an act of faith addressed to specific powers. Within this category we may group all sorts of ritual attitudes and actions from a variety of geographical locations.

For example, in some parts of the world, rituals illustrate the parents'

desire to protect the child by hiding him or her. A pregnancy may not be announced, and may even be denied. After birth, a baby may be hidden or disguised: a newborn may be blackened with soot to escape the forces that desire his or her death. A boy may be dressed as a girl in order not to arouse the envy of evil spirits. In the first weeks of life, some parents hide their babies in a corner of the house so that they cannot be followed by mythical assailants. Even though parents love their children, they may insult them, give them a demeaning name, or put them in the garbage in order to make them less appealing to evil forces. In short, the double solution of deprecation and disguise ensures the infant's survival in the face of invisible threats.

Chad.
A woman wearing
labrets holding her
child.

Many rituals reveal the parents' desire to emancipate the child. In some places, when a child begins to walk or talk, a ceremony involving washing the child's eyes takes place. This ceremony is supposed to break the deadly relationship between the invisible world, which children are from, and the world of human beings, to which children now belong. In the same vein, when the child is able to stand, the parents simulate cutting a cord that has been shackling the child, thereby enabling the child to learn to walk.

Rituals may also reflect the family's wish to prevent the "departure" of the child; i.e., to keep the baby in the world of the living. Bits of iron, or various hostile-looking objects placed by the baby's bedside, prevent spirits from capturing the baby; babies themselves are made to wear bracelets or ties made of various materials to keep them from departing for the other world. Parents may remove one shoe of a sleeping child to stop him or her from running off to the other world. These practices illustrate that among many peoples, the death of a young child is seen less as the consequence of an accident or an illness than as a voluntary act stemming from the child's indifference to the prospects of a human destiny, or from the child's discontent with the family into which he or she was born.

The methods of child rearing covered in this book are certainly different from those of the Western world. But the differences between the two are not so great when we consider that all peoples are attempting to resolve the same questions. The various solutions to our common problems are infinite in number. It is up to us to choose how we will situate ourselves, but we should respect the coherence, inventiveness, and aesthetic sensibility of those who have created other methods of child rearing.

Suzanne Lallemand, Director of Research at the
National Center for Scientific Research, France

Mali.
Tuareg women
and children.

Chapter One

Shea Butter and Calabash Bassinets

Washed, Massaged, Molded, and Painted Babies

Camel and goat droppings for the Tuaregs in Niger, a cork and a wild animal bone for the Ewe in Togo—these materials infuse the newborn baby's first bathwater with their magic power. Through this magic the baby will own large herds as an adult; will float light as a cork over traps set by enemies; and strong as a wild animal, will be able to fight against them.

Every day during the baby's first months, Indian and African mothers—like "mama bathtubs"—place their babies on their stretched-out legs, sprinkle them with water, rub them, stretch their bodies in every direction, spray them with water from their mouths, and blow into and clean all the orifices of the little body. Through the openings of the mouth, nose, ears, and anus, the baby is purged and washed on the inside. The child is healed of present and future ills by the ingredients added to the bath, the wash water, and the drinks that he or she soaks up. All this water removes from inside and outside the baby's body—and maybe from the soul as well—the pollution that he or she brings from the next world, where babies are from.

Through the ritual of bathing, the infant is reborn and gradually emerges from the world of ancestors to join the tribe to which he or she belongs. Among the Wayapis of Guyana, the mother washes her baby in a stream of water, which she warms with her mouth and directs over the infant's delicate skin. She then dries her child by blowing on the little body. Through massage, the infant's body, still soft and flabby, begins to define itself. Through grooming, often joined by massage and ritual baths, an initiation takes place: the bath purifies and the massage stimulates, firming the child's body and imparting muscle tone and flexibility, as well as virility, strength, and fertility. Makeup is applied to the baby for both aesthetic and protective reasons. The color of the beauty products, which is often black, wards off the evil eye. Makeup also ages the child artificially—by disguising the child as an adult, the parents hope to make him or her less fragile.

Niger.

A midwife gives a Peul newborn a first bath in a calabash.

Sprinkled, Powdered, and Groomed

In Niger, the Peul midwife or grand-mother performs the ritual of the new-born's first bath with a dexterity that is the result of long years of apprentice-ship. In many parts of Africa, this first bath, and each subsequent one, includes or is followed by a massage. The mother concentrates on following the proper procedure of her work: she is obeying tradition. This bath takes place in silence, without a pause, with firm vigor. Rather than being a moment of relaxation, joy-ous splashing, or play with the mother, it is one of the few times during the day when the mother lets her baby cry—loud crying is even considered a sign of good health. More than simple hygiene, the bath is considered a serious duty that purifies the baby. The bath cleanses, a vital concern in regions in which disease is never far off, but it also washes away the impurities brought from the next world. That is why the baby is washed so rigorously, and sprinkled, groomed, scraped, and soaped repeatedly.

According to the ethnologist Claude Rivière, among the Ewe of Togo, the baby is coated with a mixture of palm oil and lemon juice in order to disinfect the little body from the "pollution" of birth. The baby is then washed three times a day for a month to eliminate—before it is too late—the symbolic filth and its fetid odor. In New Guinea, Yafar moth-ers clean their babies with slightly bitter dry leaves for three weeks. By rubbing and abrading the epidermis, they there-by slough off the child's soiled skin.

Through bathing, the baby is trans-formed and reborn. Some of these first baths are extraordinary: ethnologist Marguerite Dupire reports that at the Wodaabe naming ceremony, the Peul baby is plunged by a paternal aunt into the belly of a cow whose throat has been cut as a sacrifice. Through this bloodbath, it is as if the baby is reborn from the entrails of the animal and endowed with a new life force.

Niger.
Bathing a Peul new-
born.

Kenya.
Bathing a Turkana
baby.

Herbal Baths

While Western mothers try to stop their babies from drinking the bathwater, African and Asian mothers encourage their babies to ritually drink a little from their cupped hand. Often they infuse the calabashes or basins in which babies are bathed with various plants that are supposed to keep the child in good health. First, the baby drinks a few sips of these herb baths, then he or she is liberally splashed. Sometimes, even the water the baby excretes is collected and given to him or her to drink, for strength, like an autogenous vaccination.

Kenya.
A mother soaping her baby seated on her feet.

Kenya.
The spit bath of a Maasai baby.

Spit Baths

In South America, Africa, Indonesia, and Oceania, mothers purposely spit on their children. In Guyana, the Wayapi mother fills her mouth with water, then sprays it gently over her child. In Brazil, the Kayapo mother also uses her mouth to shower her newborn. The shower techniques used by the mother vary, but they all enable her to warm the water, while at the same time symbolically "maternalizing" it. Maasai mothers direct a strong jet of water at the baby, while Batak mothers in Sumatra blow a diffused spray over their infant. As with normal baths, curative and protective plants form a part of these spit baths. In New Caledonia, women spit chewed-up herbs on the baby's fontanel; they then massage the top of the skull with this greenish lotion.

Mali.
A Dogon baby's
bath and massage.

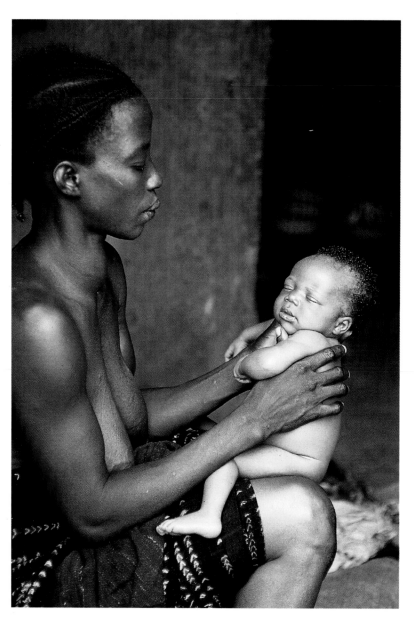

A Well-Oiled Ritual

In Mali, every morning and evening, the Dogon mother washes her newborn. She sits down on a little stool in the courtyard of her house, puts her baby belly-down on her thighs, and massages the baby with the oil of wild grapes that is kept in a small clay dish—she starts with the baby's head, carefully kneads the earlobes, then works down the length of the body, rubbing every part of the baby. She is careful to spread the shoulder blades by pulling on the elbows, and she firmly stretches the baby's legs. Finally, she washes her child with warm water from a small clay pot, before drying the child in a loincloth. This muscular grooming is repeated throughout the entire first year of the baby's life. According to the Dogons, if a baby is too skinny, it is because he or she has been badly massaged.

Smoothing Out the Wrinkles

Limbering and firming are the key words of the exercises to which "massage mamas" introduce their babies during the bath. The mother attentively observes her child's reactions, gauges muscle tone, and looks for any symptoms of illness. Through massage, she examines her child's health and makes a daily diagnosis. She pulls on the baby's arms and legs, and holds him or her up by the feet, hands, or head. She then throws the baby up in the air, to test his or her strength, as well as to teach her child to confront fear. She smooths and "irons" the baby, which comes out of the uterus hunched and crumpled up. With her heavy massage and precise pressure, she constructs and consolidates her baby, firming and joining the skeleton, and knitting together bone, flesh, and joints. If badly massaged, the child is stunted: "a badly massaged child can grow for a year before the body becomes joined together," a Gouru mother from the Ivory Coast explained to ethnologist Claudie Haxaire.

Introduction to the Heavens

Once the Dogon child has been massaged and vigorously soaped, rinsed, and wiped, he or she is finally comforted. Nadine Wanono reports that in western Africa, the baby is raised in both hands, sometimes thrown carefully into the air, and then comforted with little taps on the back and shoulder blades. *I kébé* means "the child presented" in the language of the Dogon: the infant is raised toward the sky to an invisible addressee, an ultimately divine presence. The aftermath of the bath is also a time of tenderness and play. The mother consoles her baby by offering her breast, then nestles the child against her back.

Body to Body

The mother acts as a shower-head, a deck chair, a swaddling and massage table, and a pantry. She uses all the parts of her body—mouth, hands, shins, ankles, and feet—to wash and care for her baby. To help him or her eliminate waste, she seats the baby comfortably on her perfectly angled shins, propped up on her upturned feet, and thus kept away from the mud and filth of the ground. The baby stretches out on his or her back on the mother's outstretched legs, head against her ankles, then turns belly-down like a little frog, face buried between her shins, making little gurgling noises of protest. When the mother senses that her baby needs to eliminate waste, she sits the child on her shins and makes little hushing sounds of encouragement. Thus, from one continent to another—in the absence of all baby furniture—the same positions have been invented.

India.

A mother washing her baby on her shins.

Cameroon.

A mother giving her baby a drink of washing water.

Spiced Babies

Large quantities of plants—herbs, leaves, roots, and strips of bark—often float in the basins used for washing babies. Prepared as infusions, they make the baby's bath look like a greenish marinade. They combine magical properties with antiseptic and emollient qualities, and are believed to protect the baby from the dangers of the parents' hunting. Far from being wild, animals belong to powerful spirits; thus, hunting is a perilous activity that may elicit punishment, and this punishment is often directed toward babies, the weakest link in society. Plants serve as an antidote. When brewed in the bathwater, they create a protective screen around the baby's body, so that when a vengeful spirit seeks a child, it finds only familiar plants.

Doubtless, we can view these practices as a way to welcome the baby into the world of smell, in addition to removing the odor of the hereafter. The plants and animal matter used to spice the baby— saffron, turmeric, ginger, frangipani, buffalo dung, bear grease, and sap—serve to integrate the new arrival into the clan. In Douala, Cameroon, during the ceremony that takes place after the newborn's first washing, the baby's body is rubbed with an enormous live red rooster. "The rooster is like soap; it takes away the bad smell that comes from the next world," the old woman in charge of the operation explained to Eric de Rosny.

Right: Congo.
Washing a Pygmy
baby.

34

Nepal.
Massaging a Newar
baby.

The Baby as Modeling Clay

The baby's body must be worked while it is still tender. In most societies, babies are only massaged for the first few days or weeks, and very rarely after they begin walking. The mother begins the massage with the baby's head, the most noble part of the body, and ends with the feet. Every body part has a role that is simultaneously functional, aesthetic, and symbolic. This is certainly true with the nose: in Niger, the Peul baby must have a thin nose to be considered beautiful. Among the Tuaregs, as among all Muslim populations, the mother pulls and pinches the nose, which is considered a symbol of honor. In the Amazon Basin, the Matis remold and realign the little nose, which must not be too hooked, so that the baby can wear a nasal pendant.

Massage gives the baby, still in a symbiotic relationship with the mother, a knowledge of the limits and the contours of his or her body. Above all, this muscular grooming is intended to shape the baby, and to give the child his or her eventual form and features. In the words of Jean-Paul Eschilmann, massage turns this still soft and fluid being into a "stable human compound." In Africa, the baby is believed to have an invisible double: Eschilmann reports that in the Ivory Coast, parents are afraid that this double, which is still not solidly linked to the body, may be detached when the baby is dried after the bath and left resting in the loincloth.

Nepal.
Flexibility exercises
for joints.

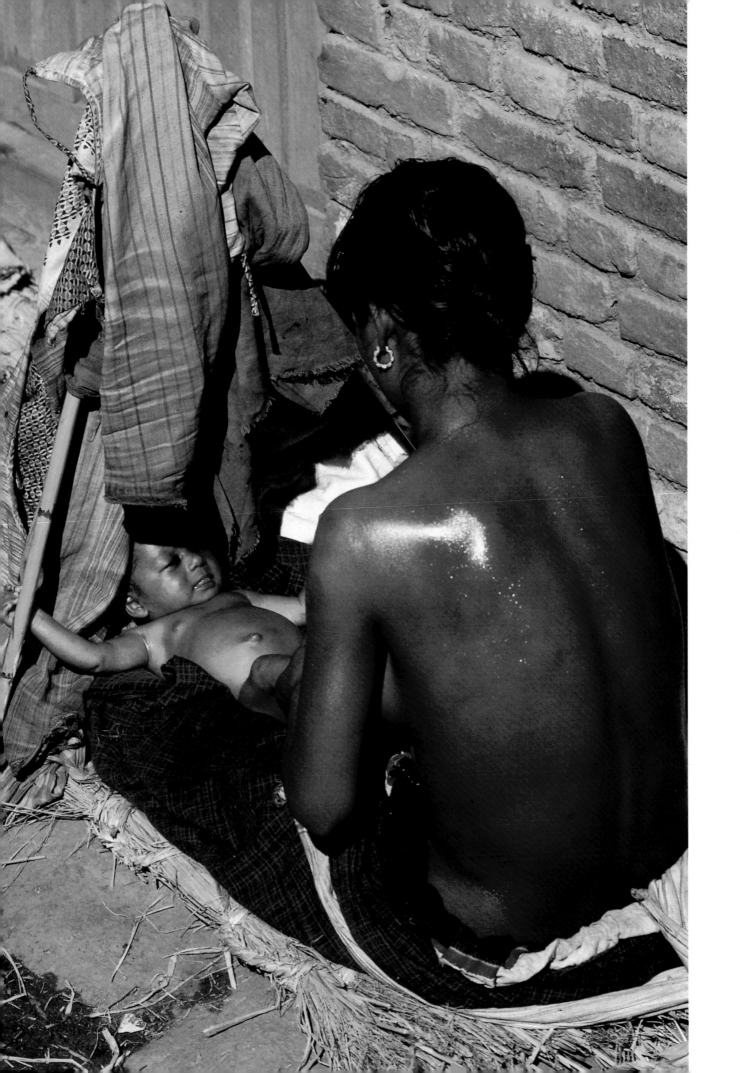

**Left and right:
Nepal.**
A mustard-oil massage for a baby sheltered under a canopy made of a tripod hung with the baby's clothing.

Oil of Mustard, Sesame, or Coconut

In those regions where dehydration and malnutrition always threaten children, nothing is more worrisome than a thin or "dried-up" baby. And nothing is more important, besides a firm and chubby body, than the skin's appearance, which should be supple, soft, and shiny. The bathwater—often supplemented with various ingredients, especially massage oils—moisturizes, nourishes, and fattens the baby's skin, making it beautiful and strong. The unction of various oils—shea tree, palm, mustard, sesame, apricot-kernel, coconut, and olive—is used to massage children and make their skin shiny, while also protecting them from the sun, dry air, and even insects.

In some regions, the baby's skin, which acts as a sponge that absorbs water, oil, and remedies through the pores, is coated with pastes, powders, or charcoal. These coatings serve a practical function by absorbing excess oil, but they also serve therapeutic and symbolic functions. In India, an oil massage is followed by an application of scrubbing powder, a mild detergent powder made of pitch or beans, or by turmeric powder, an antiseptic. Rice powder, used to dry and whiten the skin, has today been replaced with talc, which absorbs excess oil and perspiration in addition to whitening the skin. Babies' faces are liberally powdered. Among the Kabyles, a powder made of white clay is used to absorb the oil. Among the Mandan Indians of North America, heated and ground-up bison dung was used for this purpose.

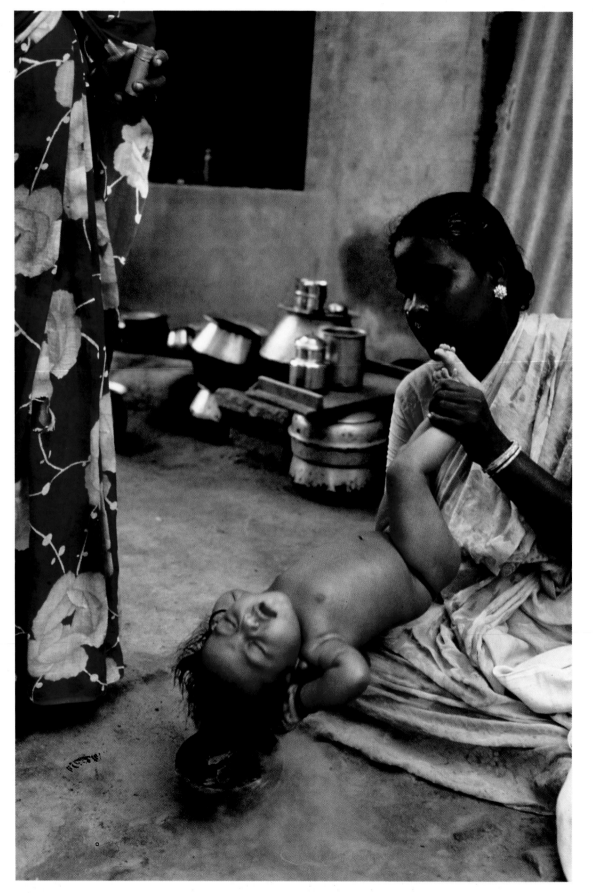

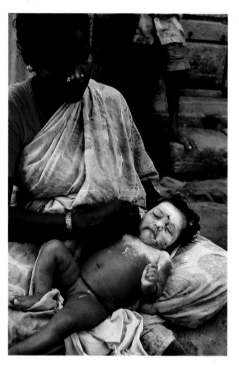

India.
The wiping, smok-
ing, and powdering
of a Tamil baby.

Mysterious Orifices

In India, as in Africa, the baby's bath is not over without a deep cleaning and inspection of all the orifices of the little body. The mother carefully inspects the openings of the passages through which the baby's vital spirit may force a path. At the end of the bath, the Indian mother blows water into the ears, nose, eyes, and mouth of the infant, in order to clear them. This clearing is probably symbolic, but in a more prosaic sense, deep hygiene is necessary as orifices are especially likely to retain impurities. In Africa, mothers blow water into their babies' noses, then put their lips around the minuscule nostrils and efficiently clear the blocked sinuses, spitting out the mucus. At the other end of the body, the mother blows a mouthful of water into the baby's anus as an enema to prevent constipation. This tradition also allows mothers to administer medicines and to check the cleanliness of these babies who have never known diapers.

Many peoples practice minor scarification on the baby's body in order to multiply the orifices by which remedies and beneficial elements from the bath may be introduced. Hélène Stork describes the ceremony of the oil bath in India, in which tea made of garlic or ginger is poured into the baby's mouth with a little bottle (formerly conch shells were used). This drink is supposed to protect the child from various troubles, facilitate speech, and promote a rich voice.

Cleaning Babies with Smoke

In many places in the world, such as Australia, Africa, and India, babies are smoked. Mothers, midwives, or healers move them gently over the hearth or a small brazier. One side of the baby—the head, buttocks, and the back—is exposed to the smoke, and then the baby is turned over like a pancake. The babies cough, shiver, or sleep. As is often the case with rituals, these extraordinary techniques of smoking serve a function that is at once magical and practical. In India, for example, particles of incense or benzoin added to the braziers serve to perfume the baby, while also drying him or her. Benzoin is known for its stimulative and antiseptic properties, but also for its strong odor, which keeps away the demons that covet children. The baby's good smell attracts demons, and the smoke serves as a screen to mask this smell. We may also interpret this passing of the infant over the fire as a sort of cooking—especially in light of the other manipulations the baby has been subjected to that strongly resemble the kneading of soft dough.

Smoking also often serves to treat illnesses. To treat a cold or a fever, the Kabyles use toad droppings, hoof trimmings, camel hair and dung, and oleander leaves to smoke babies. These leaves are associated with a specific ritual. Kabyles must go to the foot of an isolated oleander, pull down its branches, and place a large stone on the bush while saying, "I will remove the weight that drags you down when you make my child's illness disappear." Smoking is added to other techniques and rituals, which are themselves linked by secret and complicated connections, as if this complexity itself will increase their power.

Australia.
Aboriginal women
during a baby's
purification ceremony.

The Danger of the Fontanel

In every era, in every part of the world, babies' fontanels have been the focus of parents' fears. This part of the skull, the "soft spot," where the still unsutured bones reveal the pulse of the baby's heart, is universally distressing. Through this little opening situated in the top of the body, the fragile and volatile soul of the baby can vanish like invisible smoke that wafts up through the skull, as if through the neck of a bottle.

Parents have used various materials and strategies in an attempt to close this gap. In Tibet, parents spread a mixture of soot and butter on the baby's head to cement the fontanel. This forms a hard outer shell that also serves to control parasites in the baby's hair, which cannot be washed because water is scarce and could wash away some of the child's life force. In Nepal, the fontanel is massaged in order to make the bones grow together more quickly. This prevents the child's soul from escaping, and is also important because the child cannot begin to learn until the bones of the skull have joined. Among the Mouktele of Cameroon, a protective medicine gathered in the bush is spit onto the baby's head at birth, before the baby even begins breathing. In New Guinea, the Yafars spread some of the crumbly residue that's left by giant earthworms on the baby's fontanel. Listing of all the ingredients, signs, and gestures that are used to protect the fontanel would be impossible.

Tibet.
An Amdo newborn whose skull is covered with fat.

Tufts, Locks, and Crests

The lock of hair that parents in the West keep in their baby's scrapbook is a slight echo of other societies' numerous rituals concerning infants' hair. Since mythical times, hair has been considered the center of human force. For this reason, the first haircut is of great importance. Among many peoples, the baby is shaved on the day of birth, or a few days later. But care is taken to leave a few locks on the head—either just above the forehead, or on the top of the head, in the form of either a double tuft or a fine crest. Françoise Aubeille explains that in Muslim societies it is thought that an angel holds on to this lock when carrying a child away to paradise. The mark of uninitiated children, these various tufts are supposed to protect them from illness and accidents.

Shaving the baby's head is often symbolic of the desire for a clean break from the mother's uterus—hair is thought to collect and concentrate feminine impurities. Nonetheless, saving a part of the baby's birth hair is a way to retain the stamp of the mother and her life force.

Above:
Senegal.
A mother and her baby.

Left:
Guinea-Bissau.
An Ocanto mother and her baby in the Bijagos Islands.

Hair Necklaces

Once the baby's hair is shaved off, it is seldom thrown away carelessly. Among the Kisii of Guinea, it is gathered into a ball and given to the father, who puts it into a pouch for the child to wear around his or her neck. Among the Palaung of Burma, the shorn hair is burned in a hole in the ground, preferably one made by a rat or a mouse. In China, the hair is put in a red sack attached to the baby's belt, or sewn into the baby's pillow, or even mixed with the fur of dogs and cats and placed in a red paper that hangs over the crib. In parts of Algeria, the baby's head is shaved and the hair is rolled into several pellets the size of marbles, which are then hung around the child's neck. The necklace remains there until it falls off by itself.

Niger.
A Peul father and his child.

Hair Care

While the hair care and styles of babies have symbolic dimensions, they also reflect aesthetic concerns: it is important for the child to have beautiful hair. The infant's fine down is cut so that it will grow back thicker, and the scalp is massaged with various oils to stimulate hair growth. Often more unusual hair creams are used: the heads of newborn girls are spread with their own meconium so that they will have beautiful black hair, and many children. Thus, beautiful hair and fertility are linked. Depending on the child's sex, different ingredients are applied to the head.

Bernard Saladin d'Anglure relates that when a little Inuit boy learns to eat on his own, his grandfather gives him a piece of meat and then wipes his hands on the boy's hair, saying, "Here is my towel; let's wipe our hands on him so that animals will come to him without fear." Later in life, when the child has become a hunter, he wipes the blood or fluids on his hands onto his clothes in order to attract game.

Hirsute Babies

Since the hair is the center of one's life force, and therefore almost a part of the soul, some peoples do not touch the baby's head. For them it is vital not to cut the baby's hair, or even to brush or wash it. In Mongolia, the child's dirty and tangled hair is tenderly called "bird's down," and parents wait for years before cutting it. This term recalls the fledgling, the materialization of the souls of babies to come. The first haircut takes place at two to four years of age for girls and three to five years of age for boys, and marks the entry of the child into society. Relatives, neighbors, and friends all come to cut a lock. If someone important is absent, a lock is saved so that it can be cut when the person returns. Until this ceremony takes place, the baby is still partly linked with the supernatural world of spirits, with whom he or she has been communicating. In southern India, it is only after the sacrifice of the hair that the baby is capable of understanding sacred words.

Niger.
A mother and her baby in the Amdigra Valley.

Namibia.
A Himba mother
applying makeup to
her baby.

Ethnic Cosmetics

The Himba, a pastoral nomadic people, live in a semi-desert brushland of extreme climatic conditions in northwestern Namibia. Out of aesthetic concerns, as well as for protection from the elements and insects, women cover their bodies, their hair, and their babies with *otjize*, a coppery-red paste made from hematite. Reduced to a fine powder and mixed with animal grease, it takes on the consistency of a rich cream, which is then, according to Solenn Basdet, carefully preserved in little boxes made of horn, or in little purses made from bulls' scrotums. Only one deposit of hematite exists in Kaokoland, the land of the Himba, and women must walk for hours, even days, to obtain it. While this beauty cream adorns and protects the skin, the red color—as in many pastoral societies—symbolizes vitality and health. It evokes the earth, menstrual blood, fertility, and perhaps, a dress made from red cow skin; red cows are considered the strongest and most beautiful. According to African color symbolism, life begins in black, continues in red, and ends in white, the world of the ancestors. When a mother covers her body and her child's with the color red, she is inscribing them in the world of the living.

Namibia.
Himba mothers wearing large shells, symbols of fertility, and their babies wearing thick necklaces made of beads mounted on tree bark.

Brazil.
Kayapo women
with their babies.

Fresh Paint

From the time of birth, the Kayapo baby is painted with *roucou*, a vegetable substance, and blackened with smoke. In Guyana, Wayapi infants are covered from head to toe with a plant-based dye, *genipa*, to make them invisible to the evil spirits of the forest. Among the Matsigenkas of Peru, the mother covers her baby with the same substance, making the child all black and thus unrecognizable to the spirit of death.

Brazil.

A Kayapo family

Repainted Babies

Taking advantage of her child's sleep, the Kayapo mother sets herself to one of her important tasks: the decoration of her offspring. She sits in front of her house, her little one asleep on her knees, and sets in front of her two calabashes: one filled with *roucou* paste, the other with *genipa* paste. To make *roucou* paste, she rubs the *roucou* grains then soaks the pigment they contain in saliva. To make *genipa* paste, she chews the fruits of the *genipayer* tree (fruits with a very bitter flesh that provide protection against evil spirits), then mixes them with wood ash. As it takes several hours for *genipa* to actually dye the skin, the ash allows her to see the lines as she draws. Using a palm leaf as a paintbrush, she draws traditional designs that vary in complexity from geometric blocks and rays of color to complicated networks of straight or curved lines. Absorbed in her task, she carefully licks away badly drawn lines before they dry. She gives free rein to her imagination and embellishes the traditional designs of her clan. Her painting can also transmit messages, or record her mood. The designs she draws on her child may express her fury at a husband who has not gone hunting! She can allow herself to do this because *genipa* paintings wear off in a week or two. Kayapo mothers regularly devote long periods of time to repainting their babies while they sleep. If the child begins to stir, she makes a purring sound to put the baby back to sleep.

Brazil.
Kayapo women
with their babies.

54

Babies with Dots

Like many Asian babies, the Palaung child wears a mark of protection on his or her forehead. Among the Palaungs, the mother draws a sign on her baby that deflects the aggression of evil spirits. The baby seems to enjoy feeling the pressure of a finger between the eyebrows. Jeanne Cuisinier relates that among the Muong of Vietnam, the mother draws a sign on the baby's forehead as soon as she takes him or her outside in order to prevent the breath of life from escaping. This little lock on the soul also serves to mark the road back for the soul, which may momentarily leave the child.

In India, Tamil mothers draw black dots—a color that is unattractive to evil spirits and therefore drives them away—on the baby's face. A dot in the middle of the forehead or on the chin beautifies the infant; a dot on the cheeks wards off the evil eye. However, in Malaysia, the large black dot that is carefully drawn on the child's forehead is known as the *tilaka*, or "eye of knowledge," a kind of third eye. This mark, which is made on the occasion of an important ritual, illness, or change of season, promotes the spiritual awakening of the child. But not all dots are black: at important feasts in China, a baby is sprinkled with red dots, the lucky color of happiness. These dots are placed on the key features of the face, the baby's energy points.

Burma.
A Palaung woman applying makeup to her baby.

56

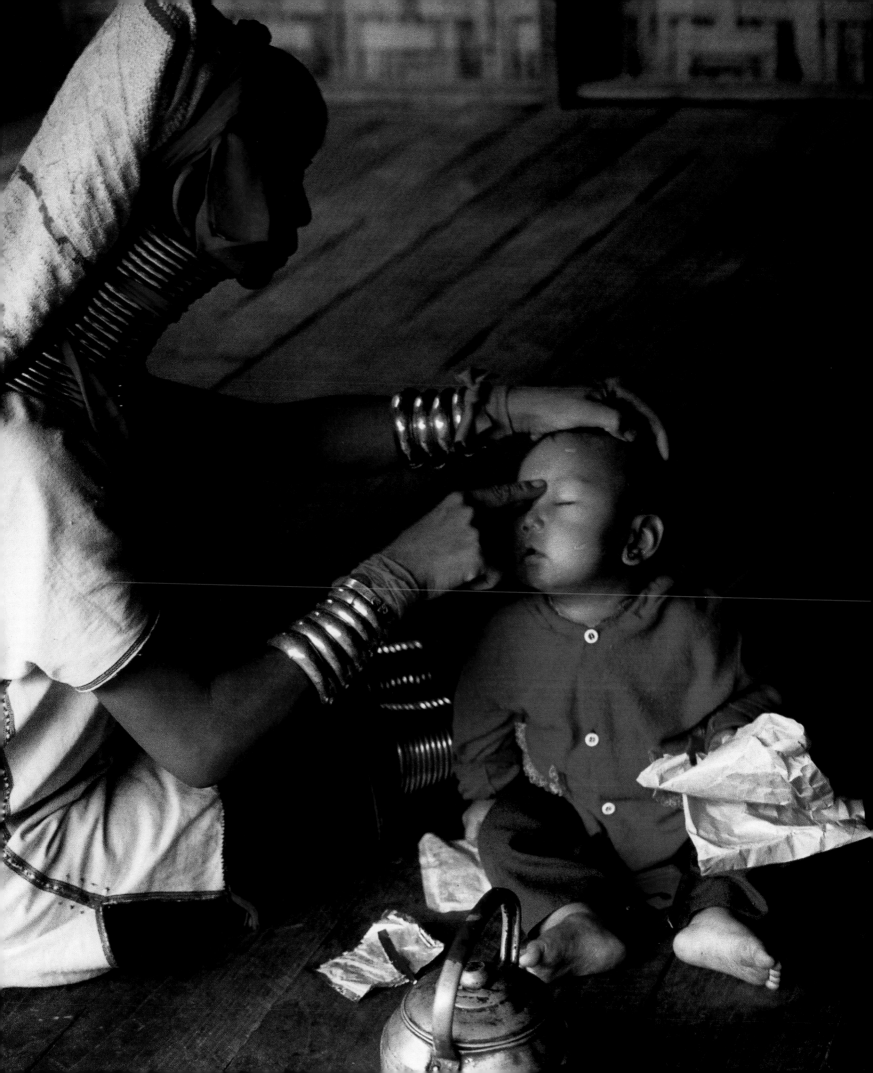

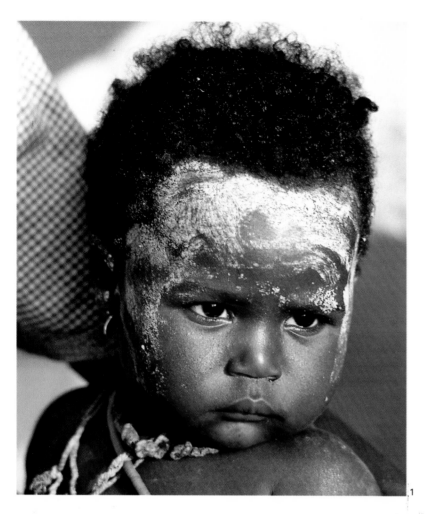

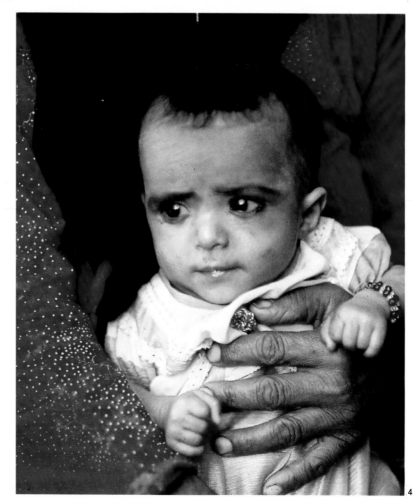

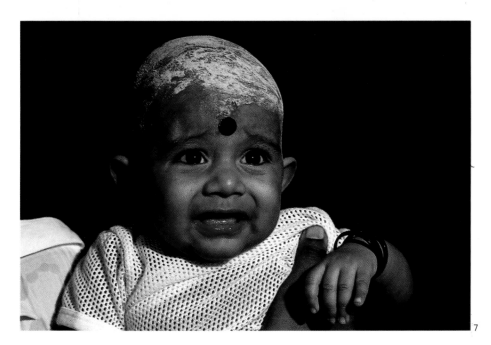

1. Sierra Leone.
2. Pakistan.
3, 4. Yemen.
5. China.
6. Nepal.
7. Malaysia.
8. Cameroon.

The Tree of Babies

Like many ethnic groups, the Onge, a people of the Andaman Islands to the southwest of Burma, use red paint for makeup. In addition to the protective powers universally ascribed to this color, these pastes also serve as mosquito repellent. The red is obtained by mixing iron oxide and animal fat in a wooden plate or a shell. The Onge also make gray, yellow, pink, and white pastes by mixing in clay of various shades. These clays are used for rituals involving mourning, initiation, and illness, but also simply to decorate the body. As in all traditional societies, having children is of fundamental importance, and all sorts of rites are designed to increase fertility. If a married man wants to have children, he must wear a band of bark around his shoulders like the one that is usually used to carry children. Women must go to a shore where a large number of stones are found; according to legend, these were once children. At low tide, she climbs onto one of these stones and the soul of the baby then enters into her body to be reincarnated. It is also thought that babies waiting to be born live in ficus trees, like a flock of birds. If a baby dies before being weaned, it again takes its place in this tree. The mother keeps the skull of her deceased baby sealed in a little basket, which she makes for this purpose.

Andaman Islands.
An Onge mother
and her child.

Chapter Two

Wolf Burnooses and Feather Loincloths

Protected, Decorated, and Swaddled Babies

Furs and skins that wrap babies up against the bitter cold, rigid swaddling clothes and minia-ture adult clothing, cords and strings of amulets—these are some of the practical and magi-cal uses of baby clothes in traditional societies. Some peoples still swaddle infants; when babies are securely tied up into a stiff little bundle, they are protected against both cold and insects, and they are easy to carry, which is important for nomadic peoples. But above all, swaddling, which holds a baby firmly in place with cords or strips of cloth, is supposed to promote healthy devel-opment of the baby's bones and limbs.

In hot regions, infants are usually allowed to remain naked. The absence of clothes can have a beneficial effect on the growth of bones, as it allows the sun's rays to reach the child. Among the Muong in Vietnam, clothing is even considered to prevent children from growing.

Clothing encloses a part of the soul and is an expression of the person; therefore, it should not be thrown away or sold, or it may inspire evil spells. Whether they are naked, swaddled, or clothed, babies in many traditional societies are adorned with jewels and amulets. Providing both decoration and magical protection, these amulets make the baby "visible," and secure the soul to the body. They protect the baby, who is still in a fragile state of transition.

Talismans such as cowries, coins, plants, religious verses, scarabs, beads, and metal transmit to the child their mysterious metaphoric and symbolic qualities. Talismans can be made of every-thing and of nothing, of materials that are dictated by tradition, or of little things that signify something to the child's parents or soothsayer. These charms, with their symbolic connections, protect the child from evil spirits and the evil eye by virtue of their material, sound, and smell. Thus, among the Mossi of Burkina Faso, the marabout makes talismans to protect the child by employing the smells that spirits are supposed to dislike. The spirit touches the necklace, smells it, makes a face, and loses interest, complaining "This child is not like us."

Siberia.
A Nenets baby in a reindeer-skin snow-suit.

Baby Clothes of Fur

Caribou, reindeer, and rabbit skin are used for baby blankets, diapers, hats, snowsuits, boots, and mittens. Babies in the polar regions live naked under their furs, which cover them from head to toe. Sometimes, when there is no moss handy, the mother uses these skins to wipe her baby. Her anorak is big enough to move her baby from her back to her breast at feeding time. If she wants to bring her baby out for comforting or showing off, she covers the baby's head with a fur hat, wraps the baby in a fold of her coat, or rolls the baby in a thick blanket, which she ties up with a piece of reindeer tendon.

As soon as the child is old enough to walk, a little snowsuit is made from a single piece of skin. In regions where small game is hunted, little suits of clothing are made from rabbit skin, or from a kind of squirrel skin that does not lose its fur or rot when it gets wet. As people from cold regions know very well that the skin of an adult seal hardens and can hurt when it gets wet, they never use it for an infant's clothes. However, Bernadette Robbe says that if, after a hunt, an unborn baby seal is found within a female seal, its supple and soft skin will be saved to make baby clothes. The trim around the hood, especially, must be made of the warmest and most caressing fur available, not only because it is in direct contact with the child's delicate face, but also because it keeps the clothing weatherproof in these regions of extreme conditions. More clothes are made for the baby as he or she slowly grows and emerges from the nest; a hood, an anorak, boots, and—the most poetic—an undershirt made of bird's skin.

Siberia.
A Nenets grand-
mother and her
baby.

Camouflaged Babies

Chukchee babies wear hats on which their mothers sew real reindeer ears. In this way, evil spirits, with their poor eyesight, will confuse them with the herd, and not steal their souls. When temperatures go below forty degrees Fahrenheit, children live naked in their fur snow-

suits, which are split at the buttocks. Beneath this split, a removable layer of leather lined with moss allows them to be changed without being undressed. The article of clothing, Joelle-Robert Lambin explains, is sewn from a single piece of skin, with built-in boots and mittens. A little opening along the bottom of the sleeve allows the child to put a hand out to play or to hold on to the mother's breast for feeding—nursing continues until the baby is two or three years old. The baby's hood, often the first piece of clothing, is made of the fur taken from reindeer legs, or from reindeer found stillborn.

**Left and opposite
page: Siberia.**
Nenets babies.
Above: Siberia.
A Chukchee baby with
reindeer's ears sewn to
his hat.

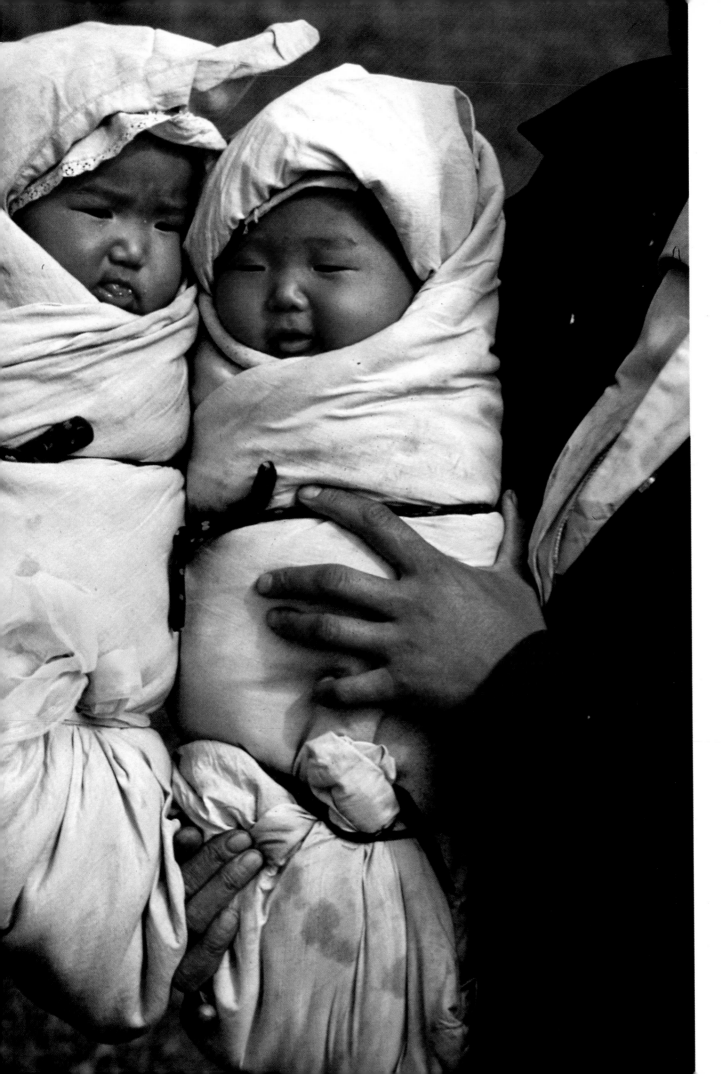

Mongolia.

Swaddled twins.

Beribboned Babies

Many societies today wrap their newborns with string like precious packages. Using various systems—crossed strings, spiral winding, or simple ties—mothers wrap their babies with sure and practiced movements. Rahmani Slimane explains in detail how a Kabyle mother wraps her baby: seated on a mat, with her legs stretched out, she arranges a six-foot-long sash, a piece of wool, and two pieces of cloth from an old robe, shirt, or veil, then puts the baby on top. After an olive-oil massage, she sprinkles her baby at the joints with powdered clay. Then she wraps the child from the shoulders to the feet, and secures the cloths by wrapping the sash around the little body. She then picks up her baby by the feet, shakes him or her gently to reestablish circulation and give him or her a long neck, and then throws the little bundle in the air.

Swaddling is also the time for ritual instructions: "I banish from you all tears, birthmarks, flaws, and the troubles of bed-wetting. Love your paternal and maternal uncles. Do not betray your origins. Be intelligent, learned and discreet. Respect yourself, be brave." A little live bird is then put into the baby's mouth for a moment so that the child will quickly learn how to talk, and will have a beautiful voice. Often, this is also the time for the love words that Nefissa Zerdoumi reports. These are never simply a matter of "my angel" or "my treasure": rather, the mother murmurs to her baby, "my little meat, my little fat, my little liver, my little honey, my grasshopper, my tiny moon, light of my eyes, little monster, my sultan."

Algeria.
Swaddled new-
borns.

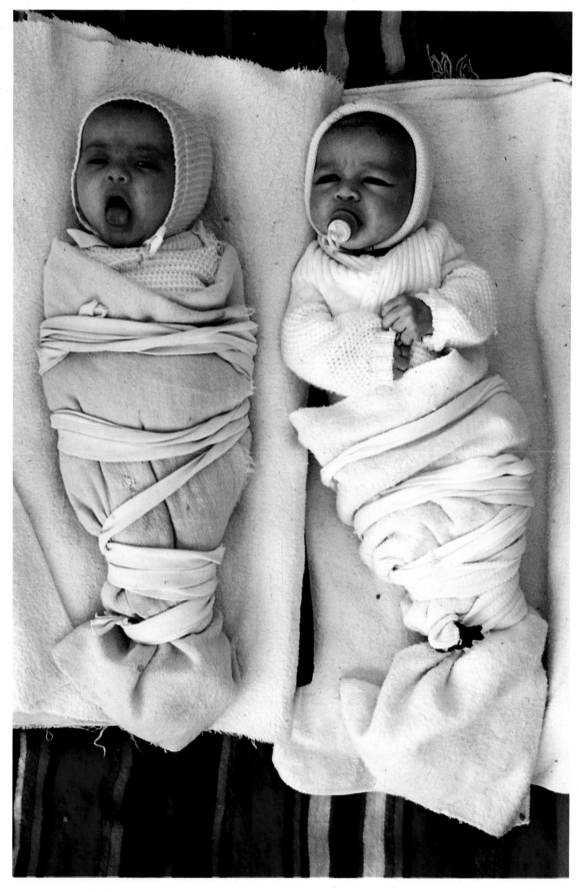

69

Tibet.
A baby rolled up
in a down-filled
blanket

Bundle Babies

Tightly wrapped in many layers of cloth, quilts, or skins, swaddled babies are nestled in their own body heat and well protected from the cold air. However, as Suzanne Lallemand notes, swaddling is not always linked to extremely cold climates; for example, many ethnic groups in central Mexico, as well as the Bataks of Sumatra, swaddle their babies. On the other hand, babies are not swaddled in Siberia; but even so, they are never directly exposed to the outside air. Infants are taken outside with only a cloth covering their face, and older children have fur-trimmed hoods, enabling them to breathe air already warmed by their own breath. In Yemen, babies are protected from the cold by swaddling and by hair stuck to their noses with a bit of fat.

China.
A swaddled baby in Xinhua.

Tibet.
A family on a pilgrimage.

At Attention

In Yemen, babies are wrapped in a long shirt before being swaddled. The swaddling is then tied with a band of printed cloth—at one time goat hair was used. To protect the baby's head, the scalp is covered with hot fat, then with a little gathered hat. While swaddling often serves to protect babies from the cold, it has always served to solidify the baby and to make him or her grow up straight with strong limbs. "Babies are frightening because they are too limp," Suzanne Lallemand explains, "so there is always a risk that they will cease to be human at any moment. To give them hardness is to confer on them one of the most reassuring human characteristics." Aristotle contrasted those people who swaddle their babies, thereby preparing them to be valorous warriors, with those who do not swaddle, thereby causing their children to degenerate into weak cowards.

Babies become so accustomed to being tightly bound that Nefissa Zerdoumi reports having seen a baby in Algeria who, put into the swaddling position, reflexively stretched out his little arms along his body in a posture of attention. He would not go to sleep until he had been immobilized in his wrappings. To protect the bottoms of these little "mummies" from moisture, mothers use various materials, depending on the region. In Yemen, swaddling clothes are lined with mucilaginous plants; elsewhere, dried and finely crumbled camel dung is often used to protect the baby from diaper rash.

This page and
opposite:
Yemen.
Swaddled babies.

Yemen.
Kohl applied to eye-
brows and eyelids
strengthen the
power of the gaze.

Claws and Feathers

Like a Christmas tree, the Yemenite baby is decorated with flounces, frills, and protective amulets, such as blue beads, fragments of ostrich feathers, family relics, and silver jewelry. The baby wears necklaces made of bits of eagle feathers that transfer their strength to the child, or long necklaces of ancient translucent amber that give the child health and a long life. Metals, stones, and minerals such as iron, copper, gold and silver, cornelian, quartz, glass, and coral have important protective powers. Animals furnish their teeth, their paws and claws, their horns and fangs, their shells and carapaces, and their skins and tails. Algerian babies wear chameleon skins and pointed teeth, which can bite or pierce the evil eye. Expectant mothers wear hedgehog paws and eagle's talons to help the fetus hold on to life. Inuit babies wear wolf bones to give them strength and endurance, and the penis bones of seals are hung from their wrists to make them great hunters.

Plants with preventative and curative properties are attached to cords that are tied to the baby or ground into powder and kept in packets attached to the baby's clothes. Children in the Central African Republic wear the bark of hard-wood trees, Dogon babies in Mali wear bracelets of baobab fiber, and Maasai babies wear bracelets from rubber plants. The Maasai also mix vegetable milk with blood, and grow a certain bean only for its fibers, which are plaited into belts for babies. Jean-Michel Mignot emphasizes the extent to which an amulet is the sum of its parts. Charms are most often attached with ties made of materials imbued with as much importance as the ties themselves.

Yemen.
A baby wearing a burlet designed to help hold up the head, decorated with buttons and a chain by the healer.

Top: Pakistan.
A baby wearing
makeup, the fore-
head encircled with
an embroidered
band.
Bottom:
Afghanistan.
A mother and her
child.

Opposite:
Afghanistan.
A Baluch baby wear-
ing a diadem.

Shaping Skulls

In some Muslim societies, babies wear a kind of headband, which is supposed to give them a large, broad forehead. For some peoples, the forehead expresses nobility, intelligence, or good luck. In Afghanistan, for forty days after birth, the infant's head is encircled with a little band of embroidered material. Since the Stone Age, people have attempted to influence the shape of the baby's skull and forehead. As in Europe during the Middle Ages, the infant's head is subjected to various massages and shapings, which may vary in intensity. The Mangbetu of Zaire and certain tribes in New Guinea employ various techniques to tightly swaddle a baby's head, such as wrapping it with strips of beaten bark, or fitting it with hats made of basketwork or frames of little boards. This cranial formatting pursues different aesthetic ends: to make the baby's head pleasingly round, very flat, or elongated.

Among some ethnic groups in Africa, it is considered good to have a very round skull, and grandfathers sometimes tease their children about their "calabash heads." These shapings also serve (like scarification) as a mark, a sign of belonging to the tribe. Also, they are supposed to increase space for the memory and for learning. According to Miya Pereira da Silva Awazu, this shaping of the skull, which has made such an impression on Western parents, perhaps originated as a way to hasten the closing of the fontanel. Another hypothesis is that the abduction of young children was commonplace in ancient societies, and a specially shaped head illustrated which tribe or social class they originally came from.

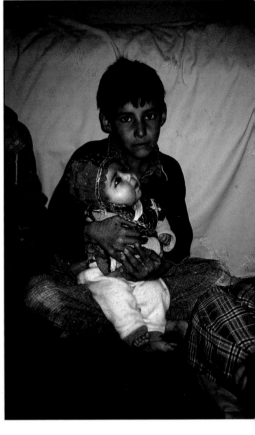

This page and
opposite:
Afghanistan.
A baby with his
mother, brother,
and father.

The Baby's Wardrobe

In Afghanistan, a month before a baby is to be born, the father goes to buy cloth so that his wife can make clothing for the newborn. Sylvie Heslot describes these baby clothes in detail: two nightshirts, six triangles of cloth, two big pieces of white material that are used to wrap the child from head to foot (one piece holds the arms, shoulders, and neck, while the other piece is wrapped around the lower body), a band embroidered with flowers for tying the swaddling, an undershirt, a headband for the forehead, and a little hat. Before swaddling, the mother spreads a coating of henna or white clay on her baby's fragile skin to keep it soft and protect it from abrasion and perspiration. She stretches the baby's legs out straight, arranges the arms close to the body, and then wraps up the child so that he or she will be solid, straight, and able to sleep without worrying about his or her hands. According to Blandine Destremeau, one of the arguments in Yemen for wrapping babies up like packages with their arms completely immobilized is that if the baby is frightened by "the world, the light, or the people," he or she may make a sudden movement, which could prove fatal. In the countryside of Afghanistan, children are often swaddled like this up to the age of one or two years.

Afghanistan.
A mother and her child.

Protective Dirt

In cold regions, and in those where water is rare, the swaddled baby is seldom washed, and then only in parts, when the face and hands are uncovered. This is due to the fear of catching a cold and of getting chapped skin, but also of evil spirits. The baby may even be left dirty on purpose to repel these spirits. Often, as in Egypt, or on the high plains of Algeria, the baby is merely wiped off at birth and is not bathed until the time of the naming ceremony seven days later. The fear of evil powers that exists in these regions compels mothers to exaggerate this dirtiness by applying kohl to the baby's face or by wrapping the baby in oily rags. In Yemen, the baby must not be washed for four or five months—this period used to be observed for a full two years—so that the child is not weakened by this symbolic effacing of the link to the mother. Françoise Aubeille explains that in Algeria, the baby's first little shirt is not washed, but folded and sewn instead into a pillow.

The diapers, which are impregnated with urine and sweat—the very essence of the baby—must be carefully protected so as not to endanger the life of the wearer. They are washed and spread out to dry in the fresh air, but they must be brought inside before sunset. If the mother forgets to bring in the diapers, she must beat them against a wall so that the baby will become as hard and solid as the wall. If the mother brings the diapers in too late, the infant is in danger of fading like the setting sun, and of being brushed against by that great enemy of babies, the bat.

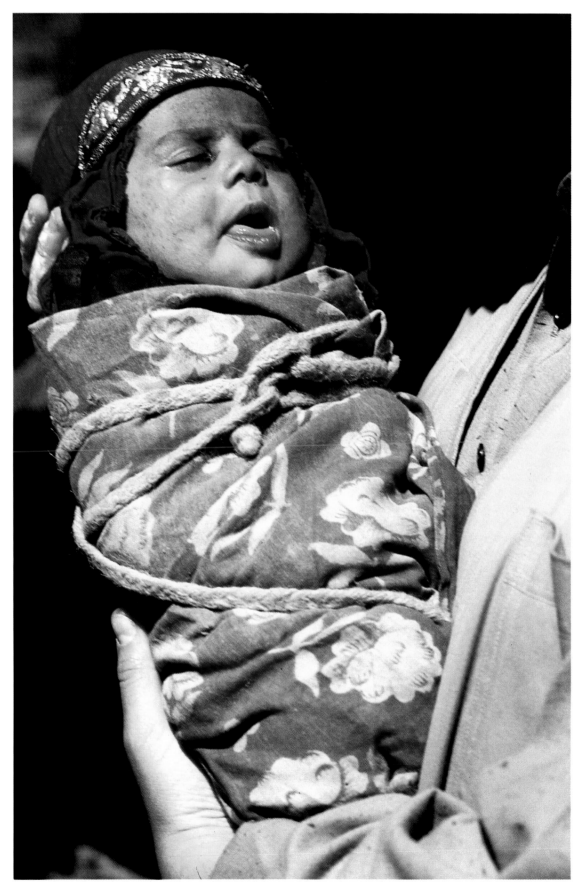

Afghanistan.
A Baluch baby surrounded by women during a marriage.

Protective Clothing

The baby rarely wears new clothes before receiving a name. In many areas of North Africa, the newborn is rolled up for the first few days in old fabric or old clothes belonging to older siblings or other relatives. On the seventh day, the day the name is conferred, the child separates once and for all from the world of the hereafter, and receives his or her new clothes, which are white, a color that symbolizes change, and communication between the visible and the invisible. Babies' clothes are often cut from old fabrics—since clothing is an extension of the individual, it confers the beneficial influence of a past wearer: the clothing of a child who escaped death may protect another who wears them. In China, parents request little pieces of fabric from one hundred prosperous families in order to make a multicolored piece of clothing for their baby. In Mongolia, when children learn to walk, they shed their swaddling clothes for a little traditional robe, which is often made of pieces of variously colored cloth. Since robes are usually of a single color, these colorful pieces of clothing are meant to confuse the spirits.

Among the Kabyles, on a child's first birthday, the mother asks for wool from seven different households and weaves a long garment, which the baby wears to guarantee a long life. In the Central African Republic, the animist priest makes a braided cord out of pieces of clothing that belonged to the newborn's parents for the baby to wear around his or her wrist for protection from spirits. These cords, fibers, and fabrics weave a complex network of ties between the baby and his or her parents, family, and neighbors.

Jangling and Clanking

Ringing, jingling, and tinkling little bells, coins, and shells drive away the evil spirits that linger around babies. The jangling of the little bell attached to the African infant's ankle keeps the enemy at bay, while allowing the parents to locate the crawling baby. The metal of the ornament protects the baby as well. Coins, bracelets, little bells, and pins are attached to babies' clothing, and knives are placed in the cradle; their sharpness and the constant, inalterable material of which they are made ward off malevolent powers.

Baby's earrings are also generally made of metal. Hélène Stork relates that in an Indian ear-piercing celebration, the priest—or sometimes the goldsmith—pierces the infant's ears in a place that has been "marked by the gods" where the skin is soft and translucent, as if "pierced by the sun's rays." The maternal uncle gives the parent gold earrings, which make the child beautiful and protect him or her from illness and evil

influences. Throughout most of Africa, as in the Andes and many other regions, the still asexual child officially becomes a girl only when her ears are pierced. But ear piercing can also have another meaning—in Nepal, the baby's ears are pierced because the gods have no taste for injured children whose blood has flowed.

India.
Anklets of a Rabari baby.

Afghanistan.
A Pashtun child.

Pakistan.
A Pashtun mother
with her little girl in
Peshawar.

Below: China.
A child wearing a hat
with tiger ears.
Right: China.
A little boy wearing
the famous Chinese
split shorts.

Lived-in Outfits

In the past, European children were dressed as miniature adults as soon as they were out of swaddling clothes. Today, in many parts of Asia, young children's clothing is often a smaller version of their parents' clothing, reflecting the belief that dressing children up as adults can fool the spirits. In Mongolia, the most fragile boys and girls are even disguised as wives for protection—they wear a costume with prominent shoulders copied from the clothing of married women. More often, a boy will be dressed up as a girl in order to hide him from evil powers. In China, hats have power because of the little ears sewn onto them that recall a tiger watching over the child. Also, a tiger's or rabbit's

head is depicted on a child's slippers, giving the slippers eyes that help to protect the child from falling down. During nap time, on the other hand, Yang Kun tells us that parents take off one of their children's shoes because they fear that if the child has both shoes, he or she will use them while sleeping to depart for the other world.

China.

A child in traditional

costume.

Drafty Pants

In China, and among the Inuit and many Siberian peoples, young children wear split pants that allow them to answer the call of nature without soiling their clothes. This clever system avoids diapers, the tedium of laundry, and the numerous changings throughout the day. If the children squat where they should not, some ashes and a quick sweep suffice to repair the damage: a stick or an old fragment of pottery can also be used to clean up the offending object, and dogs will clean up the rest. Nonetheless, even among these "split-pants tribes," the desire for cleanliness persists. Yang Kun describes the amazing celebration that occurs on the third day after birth, during which the midwife washes the baby while chanting, "Wash, wash the head / And you'll be a lord / Wash, wash the waist / You'll be a baron / Wash, wash the buttocks / You'll be a peasant!" Then she shines a mirror on the child's bottom, while reciting, "On your bottom, the mirror has shone / Do your business in the day, be clean at night." Finally, she strikes the child lightly with a leek and concludes, "One blow, be intelligent / Two blows, have a sparkling wit."

China.
A Ouighour grand-
father in Xinjiang.
Above: China.
A grandfather with
his grandchild in
1   Yunnan.

Powerful Talismans

A wild animal's tooth, some beads, a button, a small coin, a handful of fur, a pinch of nail parings, drops of blood, seeds, a holy word written with orange-flower ink, a needle, or a keyring—the ingredients used as amulets are carefully chosen by shamans, sorcerers, marabouts, or even a benevolent relative who wants to provide the child with effective protection against evil. How do these small but mighty mechanisms work? These rituals are laid down like sediment in the confines of human memory. Certain universal objects seem to be used for amulets everywhere: beads, bits of metal, buttons, and especially cowrie shells. These objects share distant origins from which they draw a part of their force: beads and prized coins, such as the famous talers of Austrian Empress Maria Theresa, come from European factories. Cowries come from the distant shores of the Indian Ocean—these little shells, shaped like a woman's sex, are the bearers of fertility and prosperity in many societies. For a long time they were used as money in Africa. Mother-of-pearl buttons, which are easier to sew and more "modern," are now often used instead of shells on garments. But buttons are not always a good substitute for cowries—in the Himalayas, cowries are attached to the baby's hat to serve as a minuscule refuge for the soul when it is pursued by demons.

Afghanistan.

A baby in Nuristan.

Beacon Bonnets

Before the twentieth century, no one in Europe went bareheaded, neither man, woman, nor child. The head, the most noble and sensitive part of the body, had to be protected from intemperate weather, as well as occult forces. Today, in many ethnic groups, women and children wear headdresses that have been carefully prepared for these same reasons. The head, which is perceived as the seat of intelligence, memory, wisdom, and learning, has numerous openings, such as the fontanel, the mouth, the ears, and the nostrils. Jewels—earrings, nose rings, labrets inserted into lips—are stationed at the entry to these openings like so many sentinels. Some African peoples think that the head

is not truly finished growing until the end of life. This is why finery and constant care are lavished on this part of the body. Thus, even in societies where hats are not worn, beads, shells, and other talismans are hung directly from the hair. On hats, bunches of objects are sometimes attached in a jumble, or—as with the Akha of Vietnam—carefully arranged. Made of many fabrics, and festooned with rows of beads, coins, and pompoms—from which an iridescent green scarab may hang—the Akha hat looks like a crown, and the baby like a little king or queen. This multicolored and jingling decorative equipment is designed as much to adorn the baby as to disorient the forces of evil.

Afghanistan.
A Pashtun father
and his baby.
Above: Nepal.
A mother and her
1   child.

Poppets with Pompoms

On the richly embroidered and ornamented hats of Yao babies, three big red pompoms blossom. Designed to bring luck and protection to the newborn, each of them symbolizes a wish for happiness: the first is the symbol of perfect happiness, the second of wealth, the third of longevity. Sometimes three cowries, or three pieces of metal—engraved with ideograms symbolizing the same wishes— are used instead of pompoms. These three pompoms sewn onto the hats of Yao babies protect them with good omens, and their red color adds a measure of protection. Throughout history, and in many parts of the world, red has been used as a color for babies. In the Andes, red clothes and amulets shield babies from the evil eye—red, which is the color of blood and thus of life, defuses the power of the evil look by drawing it to the red object and away from the child.

Colors are intrinsically powerful, and have great symbolic and therapeutic force: white protects babies, and is often the color of their first clothing; black wards off evil spirits and is used for the bracelets, belts, and collars of African infants. Finally, Suzanne Lallemand suggests that the pompoms of Yao babies provide another, more pragmatic protection: like the burlets that children learning to walk wore in Europe to protect their heads, the pompoms serve as bumpers.

Thailand.
Yao mothers and
their babies.

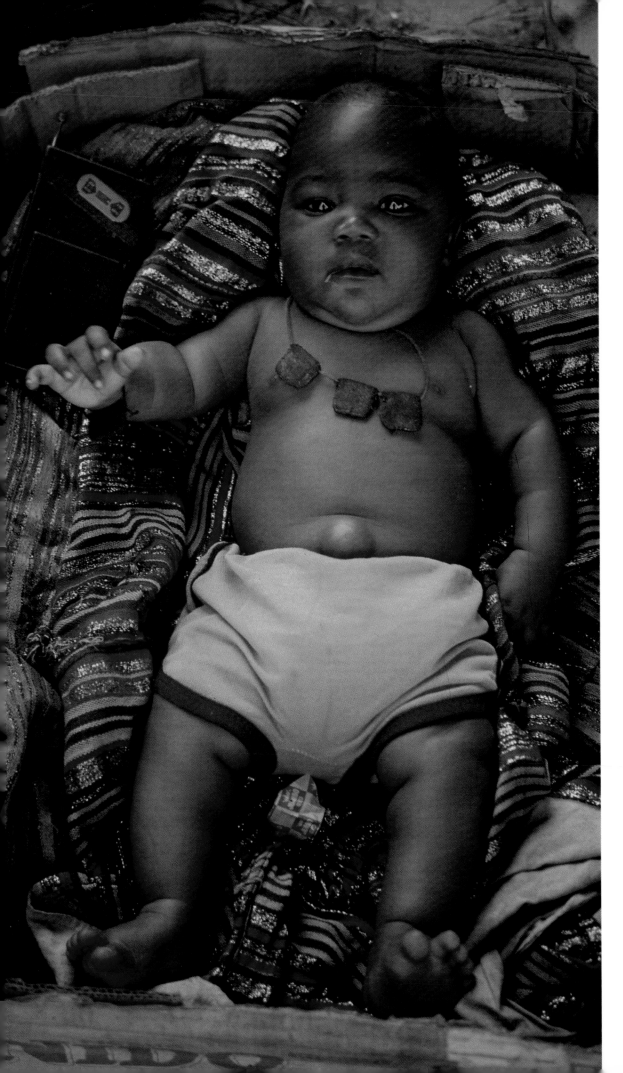

Scented Talismans

Like African adults, babies in Africa are often decorated with a garland of pouches—powdered plants in antelope horn, verses from the Koran, or magic spells sewn in little bags of cloth or leather—hung from a cord around their necks. The properties of these materials preserve the elusive virtues and powers of the talisman. Elsewhere, babies are protected by sealed amulets, the magic or religious contents of which are often kept secret so that they retain their power. They are sometimes made of materials that have an odor—sometimes agreeable and sometimes not—designed to chase away evil spirits.

One of the most pestilential amulets designed for babies has been described by Françoise Lestage: in the Andes, fathers make an amulet that their children will wear from the age of one year and that will never be thrown away. The father kills a skunk, which he cleans and fills with garlic and rue, and then sews it back up. The skunk, which secretes a malodorous liquid when attacked, is also a mythical animal, the protector of the sun and the moon. All the ingredients of this amulet—garlic, rue, skunk—have a strong odor displeasing to supernatural beings. Also, garlic is used in traditional medicine to absorb evil. A powerful distillation, this talisman serves as a false double for the baby and as a bait for evil spirits; it also absorbs dangerous influences, protecting the child from peril.

Senegal.
A baby lying in a cardboard box in Dakar.
Opposite:
Mothers with their babies.
1. Sierra Leone.
2. Niger.
3, 4. Burkina Faso.

Nambia.

A Himba grandmother with
her grandson, who is
wearing a necklace of beads
coated with red ochre and
decorated with a cowrie

Baby Anchors

Naked or clothed, babies wear thin cords of red or black, which are knotted at birth to their wrists, waists, ankles, or around their necks. Jeanne Cuisinier explains one of the most important functions of these universal strings: among the Muong in Vietnam, during the first ceremony for the baby, various spirits, as well as the new soul, are invited to come and eat. Then, the life force is invited to move into the interior of the baby's warm little body. Once the life force is inside, a bracelet of cotton or hemp is quickly attached to the baby—this is the baby's link to his or her new soul. In Yemen, the extremely tight bracelets on babies' arms can serve as reverse tourniquets, which prevent the evil spirits from making their way to the heart. These cords, chains, and jewelry are a way of handcuffing the child, or attaching the child to life on earth. Those babies who are born after their mother has lost several infants wear cascades of necklaces and jewelry, as if to weigh them down and anchor them to the ground.

Strings and knots are sometimes used in rituals for children who are in danger. Among the Mossi of Burkina Faso, Jacqueline Rabain relates that the healer measures the child with tree roots. He takes sand from the footprints left by the child, and puts packets of bark and sand under the child's bed. This ritual is accompanied by magic words that flatter the baby and persuade him or her to remain among humans.

However, sometimes these fragile beings, called "child ancestors," are seen as highly intelligent. In strictly hierarchical societies, they then pose a danger to the father, whom they risk outdoing. To break this perilous relationship, the father gives his child a bracelet of precious metal as a gesture of appeasement.

Benin.
A child wearing only amulets: an animal claw, a cowrie shell, a copper ring, and beads. A small metal paper clip is holding the cowrie.

Chapter Three

Kangaroo in a Boubou and Bamboo Strollers

Stowed, Carried, and Shifted Babies

When they go for walks in the bush, Mossi mothers in Burkina Faso are careful never to put their babies on the ground, since evil spirits could steal the child and leave a double, which would get sick as soon as she returned to the village. One might believe that most mothers in the world are afraid of this kind of trick, given the extent to which tribal babies are tirelessly carried and transported everywhere, in all circumstances. Babies are the eternal appendages of their mothers, who, like packhorses, are loaded down with firewood, cooking utensils, heavy containers of water, and babies of all ages.

While the means of transport vary depending on the location, climate, and materials at hand, they also change according to the beliefs held about babies. Among the Baruyas, a tribe in New Guinea, newborns are slipped into bags that look like mesh shopping bags. The baby is carried on the mother's back with the vine handle around the mother's forehead. When a woman travels at night, she carries her baby in front, letting the child bounce on her belly rather than on her back, because ghost mothers might sneak up from behind to offer their breasts to the flesh-and-blood baby.

Baby carriers are made from antelope skin and adorned with little bells, shells, and chimes, embroidered with beads, decorated with bottle caps, and embellished with flasks of massage oil, then weighted down with charms and amulets of every description. Mothers are like universal porters, with infinitely variable means of packing and stowing babies, whether they put them on their back in sacks of clothing, portable hammocks, or little reed panniers, or wrap them in finely woven straps of vegetable fiber, ornamented with feathers.

Cameroon.
Koma women with their
babies in carriers made
of goat skin dyed with
ocher.

Cameroon.
A Fali mother and
her child.
Opposite: Ethiopia.
A baby carrier in
Alamat'a.

Kangaroo Baby Carriers

Fitted against the curve of the mother's back or into the hollow of her hip, nestled into a loincloth or into a baby carrier made of the skin of an animal sacrificed at the baby's baptism—the African baby faces the world gently, stowed against the mother as if still in her belly. The baby carrier itself is charged with symbolism linked to maternity: in Rwanda, the same word is used for both the placenta and the sheep skin in which the baby is carried. Among the Dogons of Mali, the slings for carrying children are made from bands of fabric with a blue background that represents the amniotic fluid. This symbolism is found in many regions of the world: among the Ika of Colombia, patterns representing the placenta are woven into the slings used to carry children.

The pouch that is found on some baby carriers recalls the uterus: the hood of the Inuit mother's anorak carries the naked baby warmly against her mother's body; in New Guinea, the net bag in which babies are carried stretches or contracts like the uterus according to the position of the child. Due to this close relationship between pregnancy and carrying, baby carriers are often very important and personal objects, rarely used for more than one child. The Matis in the Amazon rainforest use fibers from a budding palm tree to make a new baby carrier for every newborn. Philippe Erikson relates how a woman, whose youngest son was twelve years old, pointed out a tree to him in the middle of the forest, saying "I made my son's baby carrier from that tree."

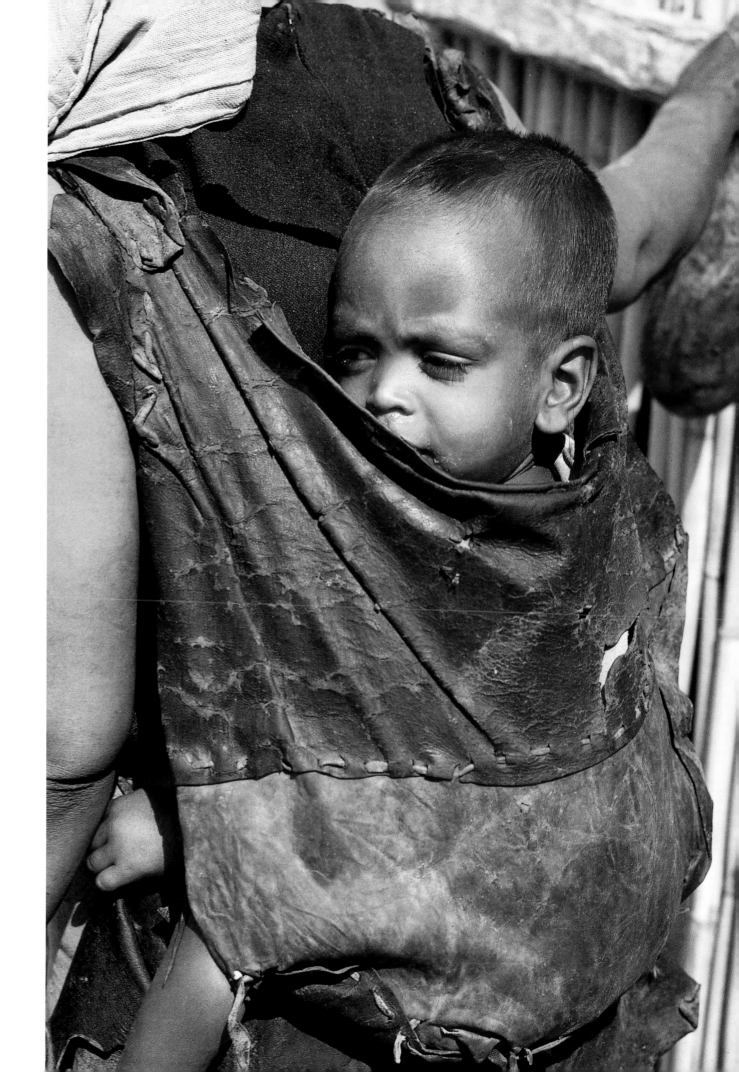

Ivory Coast.
A grandmother and
her grandchild.

Cameroon.
A Matakam woman
and her child.

Carrying and Weaning

Carrying the baby in a sling on her hip allows the mother to nurse her child at any time. Even in societies in which babies are traditionally carried on the back, like among the Arapesh of New Guinea, the child is often moved to the side so the mother can offer the comfort of her breast. The child is usually no longer carried after being weaned, which takes place at around two or three years of age. However, a sick or injured child, even if they are older, will often go back to being carried.

Depending on the ethnic group, the weaning process can happen quickly or gradually. When the end of this bonding relationship approaches, mothers often use little rituals to soften the anguish of separation. In the Ivory Coast, for example, Claudine Dubois LeBronnec and Pierre Ferrari describe the remarkable "mat game": outside front doors, in courtyards, and even in the markets, a baby seated next to a mother crawls away on all fours. At the last minute the mother catches the baby by the clothing or a foot. She brings the baby back onto the mat, while the child chuckles with joy. She lets the baby plan another escape, and, when he or she gets too far away, the mother leans down once more, catches the baby in the nick of time, and brings the child back to her once again. This game can last for more than an hour. The babies learn that their mother still exists even when they are far away from her body, and that this distance can provide pleasure.

Cameroon.

A Koma woman carrying a jug of beer on her head.

Cameroon.
A Pygmy baby
propped up in a
hole.

In the Shade of the Banana Tree

A lot of attention is lavished on the Pygmy baby. Carried by his or her mother, father, or siblings, the baby is included in all the clan's activities. The child is usually straddled over the hip and held in place by a lateral strip of cloth. In this way, the carrier can use his or her right hand and at the same time supervise the baby's well-being. Every infant is sheltered from the burning sun with a big banana leaf. For long forest journeys such as moving camp, or going on a long hunt, a carrying strap is made by sewing or knotting bark together. This strap is then placed high up on the forehead, a technique that allows older children to carry youngsters for long periods. In this way, a five- or six-year-old sister can follow her parents, who may already be burdened or busy with hunting or food gathering, while carrying her younger sibling. To keep up her strength, she may have a snack such as larvae or leftover meat carefully wrapped up in a little package of leaves.

All sorts of objects may be hung from the carrying sling, such as bits of wood for protection from spirits, or little bottles filled with medicinal oil made from palm fruit. Alain Epelboin explains that when babies are no longer carried, they may be put into a little hole in the ground, which serves to hold them upright. When children are learning to stand, canes made of the same wood used to make huts are put in the ground to help them keep their balance as they take their first steps.

Central African Republic.
Aka Pygmy children.

The Shield of Noise

A whole jumble of knickknacks are hung from baby carriers—oyster or mussel shells, beads, coins, buttons, gazelle horns, little bells, or bottle caps. Among the Bassari of Senegal, the beaded fringes on ceremonial baby carriers rattle to the rhythm of the mothers' dancing. In Borneo, snail shells beat together. In one of them is hidden the baby's dried umbilical cord. Tiger or leopard teeth, rare and costly, are reserved for the children of nobility. On some baby carriers, old Dutch coins, which have been passed from one generation to the next, click together. Among the Matsigenka of Peru, dried fruit or little plaques of pecca-

ry bone, decorated with symbols that represent the family or village, are attached to a sling that carries the baby. Marie-France Casevitz explains how this tinkling of bones, soft as the rain, calms the babies by murmuring "the song of the world" to them. The sonorous cocoon that envelops the baby is soothing and soporific. But, like the strings of beads on front doors that keep the flies out, or like those little noises that drive snakes from the trail, the little indefinable, tinkling things on baby carriers also serve to chase away the evil eye and the spirits that populate the human world.

Cameroon.
Women and children from the Kirdi tribe, a non-Muslim mountain people.

Senegal.
Initiation cere-
monies among the
Bassari.

Baby Baskets

Many factors besides temperature enter into the various means of carrying babies—the humidity, the nature of the terrain, and the mother's occupation. Often the child is carried in exactly the same way as other cargo—in a basket in Nepal and in a net bag in New Guinea. Among hunter-gatherers in the Amazon rainforest, where women need to have their hands free to pick up roots, fruit, or small animals, babies are carried with a band over the head. Baskets attached to her belt allow the mother to carry large weights—food as well as children—over the rough terrain deep in the rainforest.

In Central Africa, in parts of the forest where burdens are carried in big baskets on the back and supported by a strap across the forehead, children are wrapped in a loincloth or carried on the hip. According to Blandine Bril, on the plain it is possible to carry loads on the head, and babies on the back, because the ground is level and the load is not likely to be shifted by broken terrain.

Mali.
A Dogon mother
and her baby.

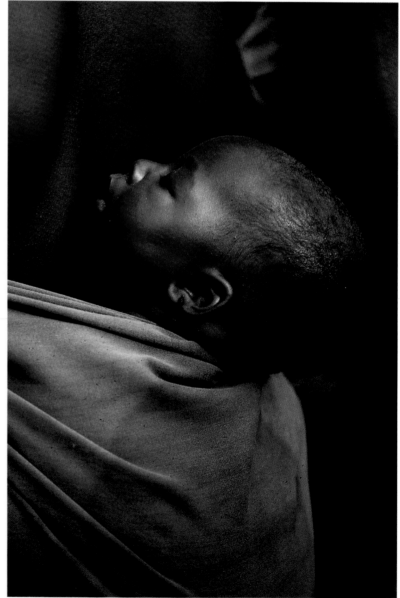

Burkina Faso.
A sleeping baby
with a lolling head.

Mali.
Dogon mothers and
their babies.

Baby Bags

In New Guinea, men and women always keep their bags with them. Made with the fibers from the aerial roots of palm trees, these sacks accompany people from the cradle to the grave. Babies, little animals, fruit, vegetables, and tools are all shoved inside. At birth, the baby is stuffed inside the sack, like a handful of potatoes. The mother carries the sack on her back, the handle around her forehead. For newborns, she is careful to line the bottom with pieces of cloth or leaves that are as soft as flannel. When the sun shines too brightly or the rain falls too hard, the precious sack is covered with a banana leaf or a cape of bark. Sometimes, the mother carries several of these string bags filled with bananas or tubers. She carries the bag containing her baby on her belly and the other bags on her back.

When traveling at night, women always put their babies in front, haunted by the fear that ghost women with full breasts will offer the baby their deadly milk. Before feeding her child, the mother always spurts some of her milk on the ground to purge the dangerous traces that the ghost mothers or their dead babies could have left while suckling undetected during the night. After a death, the string bag of the deceased is hung on the grave. Sometimes the body will even be attached upright to a beam, with string bags containing all the deceased's possessions attached to the body.

This page and
opposite:
New Guinea.
Papuan babies in
net cradles.

New Guinea.
Babies in their net
nests.

Hide the Baby

For a Baruya man from the mountains of New Guinea, his baby is an unclean thing because it is too closely linked with the pollution of birth and the dangers of the feminine world. The mother must hide the infant's face from her husband until the baby begins teething. When her husband is present, she covers the baby with her string bag, and if he happens to see the child, he spits on the ground.

Nonetheless, with the birth of each child, the man's status increases, and an astounding ceremony takes place. Maurice Godelier has described it in detail: the new father goes to wash in a river, then crawls through a tunnel of leaves. When he comes out, the older men await him to rub his abdomen with nettles. Then they give him a package of yellow mud and shout, "What's that? Earth to paint yourself with, to make you handsome? No, it's the crap of the baby that has just been born. Until it hardens you will not make love. You have been on the women's side, now we're taking you back to the men's house. Think about this child, think about making gardens for the mother and child. When your son walks and plays with a little bow, when your daughter carries a little net bag on her head, then you can pull out your penis, too."

New Guinea.
A Yafar baby whose wrists are attached by a cord to prevent falling.

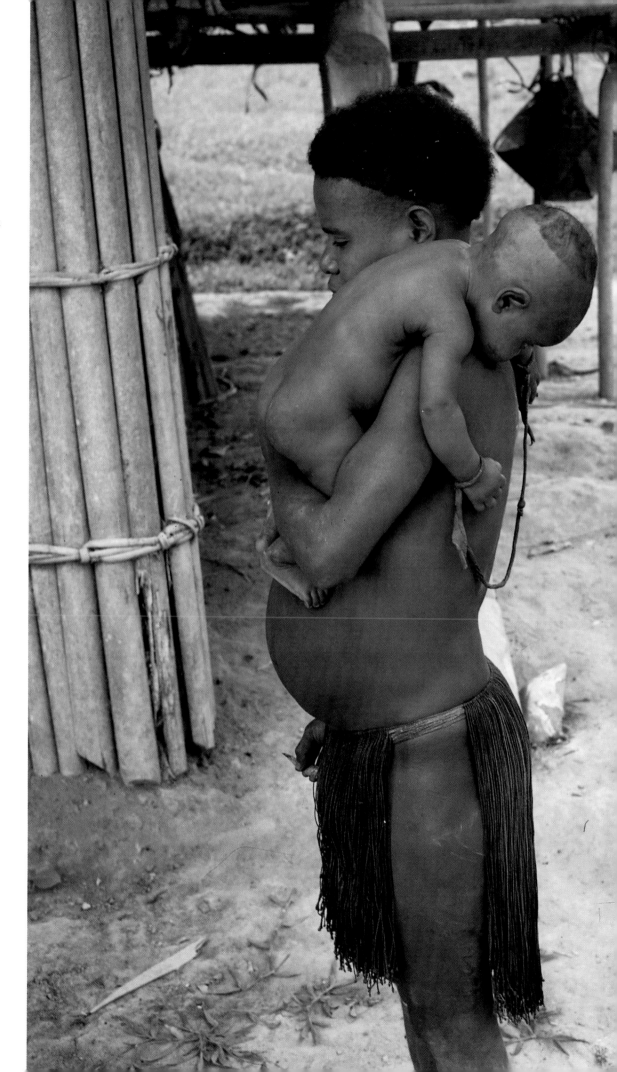

Leaks and Accidents

Among the Yanomamö in the Amazon rainforest, the infant lives like a parasite on the mother's body. It is only after children are completely weaned, usually at about the age of four, that they stop sleeping with their mothers and are given a personal sleeping hammock. The heat of the hearth is then supposed to replace the warmth of the mother's body. "There is a sort of indefinable continuity between the two," explains Jacques Lizot, "which makes separation more of a transition. But the fire is a living domestic element, and its constant presence is quasi-human." While it is rare to see a woman in Africa soiled by her baby, the Yanomamös wipe up the traces that their children leave on them without comment. Africans, however, seem able to detect the slightest signals of their children's toilet needs. At the most subtle movement or change of breath, they understand the message and take them off their backs and put them onto their ankles in an instant. If an accident happens, the mother is ashamed and embarrassed.

Some ethnologists qualify the commonly held belief that in Africa babies' bowel movements do not provoke revulsion. Nadine Wanono points out that long deodorant necklaces of cloves are worn by the mothers of young children, and Suzanne Lallemand reminds us that in many traditional rural societies men complain about these smells. In central Togo there is even a song with the refrain "To smell as bad as a woman who has a baby."

This page and opposite: Brazil. Yanomamö babies in the Amazon are carried in slings of rough or woven bark.

Against Wind and Sun

According to Dominique Champault, in most of the countries of the Maghreb, mothers do not use any baby carriers at all. Either the mother rests the baby horizontally on her back in a pocket that she makes in her robes, or she keeps the baby flat against her back, held in place by a fold of her garment, or by her scarf, or veil. But before the newborn goes outside, he or she is first prepared for the experience of being carried. Among the Tuaregs, the child is attached on a little leather cushion with a shape that is reminiscent of a back. After being cradled for a time on the cushion, the baby is ready to go outside, and to be carried on the mother's back. This carrying, which is sometimes uncomfortable, initiates the child to the conditions of life to come. Nefissa Zerdoumi writes of babies in Algeria: "The mother's back or the brother's hip, which rock and move around, are already a slightly harsh cradle for the newborn who will soon be faced with bad weather, rain, and sun."

Niger.
A Tenere baby in a little portable leather hammock.

118

Morocco.
A young Berber
woman and her
baby.

Nomad Babies

In Arabia and Yemen, baby carriers made of sheep or goat skin are sometimes treated with saffron or turmeric, which dye and perfume the skins. These spices give the infants an odiferous protection from spirits, and the infants become accustomed from their earliest days to the smells around them. A more prosaic reason for this "spicing" is that the scents deodorize the leather when it is wet with urine. In the past in the West, certain materials were also used for this purpose: small cradles constructed of pine wood had a resinous smell that was supposed to keep the baby's lungs clear while scenting the air. Carrier cradles are conceived as little protective shelters for babies. In Siberia, children are put into cradles of birch bark, which are then slipped inside giant "slippers" of reindeer skin that may be set down on the ice or snow.

In Arabia and Yemen, the baby carrier looks like a traveling bag with a clasp made of two sticks. Since only the baby's toes stick out, the cradle protects the baby from the blinding light of the desert, and from wind and sand. Hanging this sack from a wall, a tree branch, or a tripod transforms it into a cradle or a swing. Made from leather or bark, these portable cradles are very light, and the baby is no heavier than a baby swaddled in a skin or a blanket. The mother can nurse without taking her baby out of this protective shell. Sometimes she even nurses her child in the cradle while it is still hung from the ceiling.

Saudi Arabia.
A Bedouin mother with her child stretched out in a cradle carried on the shoulder.

Yemen.
A mother rocking
her baby in a cradle
hung from a
wooden tripod.

Porter Mothers

Capable of carrying tins full of water, firewood, harvest, fabric, and, resting on top of it all, a baby, mothers are remarkably strong and tough porters. Adept at changing their gait, mothers quiet their walk when they feel the baby's head start to nod, a sign that the child is asleep behind her. In the Himalayas, the Andes, and elsewhere, women who sell their wares at the markets by mountain paths and who do not own pack animals are obliged to act as porters to carry their merchandise and their children.

In Cameroon, Koma women climb like goats over rough ground with heavy jugs full of mildly alcoholic beer perched on their heads, small sips of which they give to their child. Holding themselves proudly, they smoke their pipes while carrying forty to fifty pounds on their heads, and a twenty- or thirty-pound child on their backs.

Nepal.
A mother with her baby in a basket designed to carry heavy loads.

India.
Mothers with their babies stretched out in portable hammocks.

Nepal.
A Newar baby.

From the Poles to the Equator

According to Blandine Bril, there is a geographical pattern to the manner of carrying babies: in regions where it is warmer than 50 degrees Fahrenheit during the winter, they are often slipped into African-style loincloths or carrying belts. Elsewhere, they are often swaddled, carried in cradles, or wrapped in cloths or blankets in a basket. In the Andes, the tightly swaddled baby is wrapped in a blanket knotted at the mother's breast. Here, it is the material of the baby carrier that is different from what is used in Africa—the thick blanket replaces the light loincloth, creating a warm microclimate.

India.
A Ladakhi mother
and her child.

In the Fields, at the Market, At the Fair

The Sherpa mother hardly ever leaves her baby: she sleeps against her child at night and brings the child everywhere with her during the day in a bamboo cradle, that is fastened to a strap she wears around her head. According to Gisèle Krauskopff, at every birth the Sherpas make a cradle that will not be thrown out until the child is one-and-a-half or two years old.

African mothers carry their babies to the fields, the market, on visits, and to dances. The baby is hauled around everywhere, in the sun and the rain. Grinding, winnowing, sorting, sifting, washing dishes or clothes—the child accompanies the mother in all of these activities. Voices and laughter, the dull noise of the pestle, or the clicking of the charms attached to the baby carrier—nothing prevents young babies from sleeping peacefully if they feel the need. When their mothers let them crawl on the ground, nothing prevents

them from chasing the chickens, pigs, or young goats, or from playing with their mother's cooking ingredients and utensils such as pestles, knives, fruit, cassava, ashes, dirt, wood, and water. It is rare for anyone to offer the child an object, or to play with the child, but found objects provide a useful apprenticeship for future family or social life.

However, there are countries where mothers hardly ever carry their children, and where they hardly ever take them out to work. Dominique Champault says that in Yemen, mothers rub their babies with milk when they leave for work. This milk provides the nourishment, presence, and odor of the mother, and thus reassures the baby and promotes growth. Then the babies are swaddled and left for hours with a grandmother, an older sibling, or simply alone. Sometimes, to protect the baby, mothers set up a little tent of white cotton.

This page and opposite: Nepal. Sherpa mothers in the fields with their babies in portable cradles.

Nepal.
Tibetan children.

India.
Children in Zanskar.

Opposite:
Vietnam.
A Muong father
with his children.

128

Saddle Cradles

When pastoral peoples move their flocks, the baby is stowed in the mother's arms, perched on her saddle, securely swaddled, or even attached directly to the saddle or the animal's neck. Sometimes the child is tied into a little portable cradle, the shape of a wooden shoe, and fastened to the animal's side. Finally, the baby may be slipped into a little bag, or put in a basket, a kind of saddle-cradle made of wicker. The yak, camel, donkey, mule, and horse are a few of the animals to which children are attached. Among the Lapps, the cradle is hung from the left side of a reindeer's saddle with a sack of flour or another cradle as a counterweight. Compact, and enveloping, saddle cradles keep the baby solid and safe.

These cradles have inspired many anecdotes: one tells how the strap that held the cradle to the reindeer broke. In spite of the fall, the baby inside was unhurt. Another tells how an animal bolted and disappeared into the country-side for several hours, but the parents eventually found their child safe and sound. Last of all, after a boat had cap-sized, a baby was found inside a cradle that had floated and been carried by the wind back to shore.

China.
Cane baskets can carry babies as well as supplies.

Dung Diapers

In addition to transporting a child, animals have many other uses. Yak hair and finely powdered camel dung provide the perfect absorbent materials for use as babies' diapers. Reindeer ears sewn to the children's caps offer protection from evil spirits, which will mistake them for livestock. Children's clothing is made from the skin of young reindeer, and in some Siberian cultures, the reindeer's hair is used to stuff the little fox or rabbit skin cushion that supports the baby's head.

In regions where there is little wood, yak or camel dung, which is flammable and brings good luck, feeds the fires and keeps off the spirits. Hair, claws, and teeth from bears, wolves, and monkeys are kept in pouches or hung from cords, and serve as amulets. Among the Kabyles, a boar's tusk is kept in a little bag with the umbilical cord. Like a watchdog, it is supposed to bark as soon as a spirit comes close to the baby. Among the Inuit, bird skins are sewn together to make the infant's first nightshirt.

In some Siberian tribes, the baby's coverlet is made from the skin of the heads of twenty-five ducks, or from the skin of a swan. The neck of a swan, or of a goose, is filled with pebbles and serves as a rattle for the baby. In the Amazonian rainforest, bird feathers, like sensitive antennae, detect the passage of the spirits.

Tibet.
A child swaddled and attached to a yak.

Siberia.
A Nenets baby in a
cradle on a sleigh.

Babies' Hoods

Among the Inuit, a very deep hood is used as a baby bag and serves as an extension of the womb. The newborn lives in a heated climate, completely buried inside the mother's clothing, and curled up like a half-moon. As the baby grows, he or she is installed upright and emerges from the hood little by little. A strap allows control over the height of the child, who is seated comfortably, as if in an armchair. When the ground is icy or wet, or if there are animals that might harm the baby, carrying the baby on the back is a way to keep him or her safe. This carrying also allows the mother to feel her baby. She knows her baby is warm, moving, and living. When she feels that her baby has to urinate, she takes the child out of the hood, often with the help of another woman.

According to Bernadette Robbe, when the mother goes on a long trip, she slips lichen or rabbit skin into her anorak to serve as a diaper. There is not one specific material that is always used—mothers take what they find, according to the season. In spite of the restrictions of the region, each woman is inventive enough to improvise solutions, which are then repeated if they work well. However, the baby is not always put into the mother's hood—in some areas in the East Asian Arctic, when the weather is nice and the women sit outside to sew or just talk, they slip their babies into their large waders. With only his or her head sticking out of these seven-league boots, the little one begins to discover the world.

Greenland.
An Inuit woman carrying her baby in a seal-skin anorak.

Good-Luck Charms

In China, children are carried in baby carriers made of padded cloth, which represent months of work. According to Bernard Formoso, the materials used to make them, and the colors and the designs embroidered on them, all have a very particular meaning. Each design has symbolic value. Many wish the child a happy life, and contain symbols of happiness such as butterflies, ducks, birds, and flowers; symbols of fertility such as the dragon and pomegranate; or symbols of longevity such as the lotus. Other shapes are designed to protect the baby: leaves guarantee good health and prevent snake bites in areas where these reptiles are numerous and dangerous.

Patterns may vary according to the child's gender, age, or social status. The designs are highly influenced by the culture in which the people live. For example, the designs on the baby carriers of the Yi Axi of China—a people who cultivate rice in terraced paddies—match those on the mother's clothes, and represent a stylized miniature landscape with the sun shining on the tiered rice fields and the mountainside. In the Andes, a design of embroidered zigzag lines means that the child's mother comes from the mountains. But it is not always easy to decipher the symbolism of materials and colors. An ethnologist who did research in a little village in the Andes conducted a study on the color of the scarves used to carry babies. Why did some women use a brown scarf while others used a white scarf? After researching such factors as differences in social status or religion, and after a great deal of trial and error, he found out the answer from a village woman: the mothers who wore a brown scarf owned brown sheep, while the mothers who wore a white scarf owned white sheep!

1. An Ainu baby in Japan.
2. A Chinese baby.
3. A Yi Axi baby, Yunnan province, China.
4. A Bai baby, Yunnan province, China.

China.

A Yi Axi baby in the
Guizhou province.

Porter Fathers

In Asia, fathers gladly take care of their babies. The tasks of family life are carried out indiscriminately by the father or the mother, according to their availability. Cleaning, carrying, and soothing babies is not the responsibility of the woman alone. However, in many societies fathers carry babies in their own particular way. In the Amazon rainforest, many fathers carry their children on their shoulders, while mothers carry them in front, or on their backs. In Africa, men do not carry children on their backs with the help of a loincloth, but simply hold them in their arms. Among other peoples, such as in New Guinea, there is no chance of the father doing the carrying—in the Andes, it can even mean that his wife has left him.

But even in those places where the carrying is reserved exclusively for women, parents often make the baby carriers for their infants together. The mother does the weaving and the father engraves the little bone tablets that are hung from the cloth. Elsewhere, such as among the Bassari in Africa, the father makes the baby carrier out of antelope or goat skin while his wife is pregnant. Among the Koma of Cameroon, the father makes the carrier, and then has the task of keeping his wife supplied with fresh leaves so she can make the little tuft that hangs under the carrier and hides the baby's bottom. If the leaves are not fresh, there will probably be a family fight! In Java, it is not the father's job to make the scarf in which the little one is carried, but he is given a red-and-white scarf in which he will take away his wife's placenta for burial.

China.

A father carrying his child, who is wearing a "tiger hat," designed to chase away evil spirits.

Babies in Palanquins

Baby carriers, which are often richly decorated with weaving, appliqué, stitching, and embroidery, are the fruit of long hours, or even months, of work. Depending on the region, the parents or the grandmother usually begin work on the design well before the child is born. But among many ethnic groups, the baby is carried by whatever means are at hand, just like other loads. For example, all over Asia, little children are carried by means of the portage pole, which consists of two baskets hanging from either end of a long pole. Used to carry rice, earth, and all sorts of things, this device allows for even distribution of weight, making it an easier way to carry two children than in the arms. When it comes to carrying, it is always a matter of adjusting the weight so that the burden does not become too heavy. The height of the bundle on the carrier's back, the width of the straps, and the position of the belt across the chest or the forehead are all important.

China.
A Miao mother and
her babies in the
Guizhou province.
Above: China.
A father carrying his
baby in a bamboo
1 structure.

Burma.

A child in a walker.

First Steps

In China, the baby's first steps are considered to be a very important moment in life. But, like every baby learning to walk, falls are common. According to popular belief, if a child wobbles like this, it is because the feet are still tied with a cord dating from his or her former life. In fact, when someone dies, the ankles are tied together with hemp, lest the corpse rise up and haunt the living. In order for the baby to walk freely, it is necessary to get rid of this binding. In some regions, the parents place a straw cord under the baby's feet, and cut it three times with a meat cleaver. In Mongolia, parents pretend to cut an imaginary shackle between the child's feet. Among the Ewe of Togo, a stream of water is poured between the child's legs so that the child will be able to run as fast as a stream. In Central Africa, short and rhythmic "walking tunes" encourage the child to run forward.

According to Marie-France Adrien Rongier, women speak of their babies in terms of the development of their motor skills: "How's your baby?" "He's fine, he's standing up straight." These stages determine social growth, indicate the child's age, and influence the parents' social status. "That woman has a boy who's walking," "That woman's son has a baby who's already sitting up"—the baby's progress inspires the admiration of the village folk for the parents or grandparents who have raised the child. Among the Bassas of central Africa, parents also attach a great deal of importance to the first step, and they watch for the most agile foot: if the right foot—the one on the masculine side—is more nimble, the father is proud and the mother is irritated; if it is the left foot, the mother is proud.

China.

A baby in a bamboo
stroller in the
Szechwan province.

China.
A baby sitting in a
wooden keg turned
into a baby chair.

Planted Babies

In China, parents rig up wooden buckets into which they put children who can already stand up straight; or they make special devices that are raised above the ground like little watchtowers. In other places, such as in Africa among the Pygmies, or in the Andes, the infant is wedged into a hole in the ground, from which he or she cannot escape. In Peru, the mother carries her baby around everywhere. When she has to work, she digs a hole—called a well—in the family courtyard or the field, and puts the baby inside, wrapped in a blanket. In the rainy season, the hole is replaced by a tin bucket lined with blankets.

Françoise Lestage wonders what allows mothers to entrust their babies to a hole in the ground, when most peasants are afraid that the earth will seize babies, or steal their life energy. These feelings of ambivalence toward the earth are common in the Andes, as well as many other parts of the world. However, it seems that the earth, the baby's first mother, also has the same ability as a human mother to protect the child. When the baby is planted in a hole, he or she is nourished by the earth like a stalk of corn or a potato.

Chapter Four

Coconut Matting
or Reed Cradles

Babies Suspended, Rocked, Shaken, and Comforted

"My little chatterbox, Kanama, my treasure, you came into the world to ease my pains, you bring me happiness," an Indian mother hums while vigorously rocking her baby in a hammock made from one of her old saris. Calmed by the melody of a lullaby, little rhythmical pats on the back, and the rocking of the cradle or arms, babies fall asleep surrounded by family. Snuggled against the mother, or in the midst of parents, grandparents, and brothers and sisters, the baby is sheltered from the evil powers. Comforted at all hours of the day and night by their mother's breast and the caresses of relatives, babies are not supposed to cry. Perhaps because the baby is still halfway between this world and the next, crying echoes like a distress call to the spirits of the other world who could summon the baby back to them.

Curled up on a loincloth, a mat, or a tatami, nestled in the cocoon of a hammock made of fabric, leather, or fashioned from an old rice sack, stowed in a wooden cradle hung from cords or sitting on a tripod, the tribal baby sleeps peacefully. Even when the cradle is empty, it is the object of a thousand precautions: the Kabyle mother is careful never to rock the empty cradle, for fear of causing her child's death; in the Comoros Islands when a child is taken out of the cradle, the mattress is quickly turned over so that a spirit cannot slip into it, attracted by the warm bedclothes and the baby's good smell.

Siberia.
A Nenets mother
rocking her baby.

147

The Sleeping Soul

Among many peoples, sleep is a moment when the soul may escape and travel to the world of the supernatural. A child who begins to laugh or cry at the moment he or she falls asleep is, without a doubt, in the presence of a spirit. In Mongolia, it is believed that a fox is telling the baby a story, pretending that the mother is dead. When the child then starts to wail, the animal admits that it is all a trick and the little one then laughs from relief. This is why babies may have trouble falling asleep and why they have joyful little smiles flitting over their faces when they sleep, like airy clouds in the skies. "I saw a mother," Catherine Aballea relates, "who gently but firmly closed her baby's mouth during sleep because there is always the danger that the soul will slip away through the body's orifices." Among the Inuit, there is a sleeping soul that does leave the body, and that causes sleep. It leaves and returns by the anus, the door of the soul. And if some people, when they awaken, speak incoherent words, it is because their sleeping soul has not had time to return to its home. That is why one must never awaken a sleeping baby too quickly.

The human body is the recipient of a multitude of small souls, explains Paul-Emile Victor. The child is born with a life soul, a sleep soul, and linking souls. But the most important soul is missing, without which life is not possible—the name soul, hardly as big as a snow sparrow. Before the baby is baptized, this name soul, which has just left another body, waits somewhere in transit, shivering with cold. As soon as it hears the call, it rushes to the newborn's house and enters the baby's body. Thankful, it curls up in the warmth, at the base of the neck, next to the life soul. The sleep soul lives in the groin and is no bigger than a flea.

Mongolia.

A mother rocking her baby with a string.

149

Camouflaged Baby

As an infant, the Afghan child is placed on a little mattress. Sometimes the father makes a little arch of willow, and places it above the child's head. A cloth is placed on this curved branch to protect the baby. But the newly born infant is simply put on the ground and covered with a piece of canvas. Sylvie Heslot warns that one must be very careful not to step on a baby when entering a house, because it is easy to mistake one for a cushion or a pile of rags.

Closed Beds

A few weeks later the baby is put in a poplar bed. Decorated with protective colors, this bed is a regular little house. The baby is tightly swaddled and tied to the bed with string. Two wooden arches above the child's head and feet are joined by a stick or cord, on which is spread a quilted blanket that protects the child from the cold, insects, noise, and light—but also from evil spirits. This arrangement can also serve as a handle that allows the cradle to be moved or carried more easily.

Miniature Urinals

How is it that the Afghan baby, with no diapers, does not live in a permanent state of dampness? Sylvie Heslot describes how the child is arranged and swaddled, with the legs perfectly straight, clasped around a little wooden tube that serves to collect the urine. Different urinal models have been adapted for boys and girls. Thanks to this ingenious drainage system, urine runs into a little bowl placed under a hole made in the bottom of the cradle. The wooden tube is sometimes replaced by a bit of bicycle inner tube that leads to the urinal.

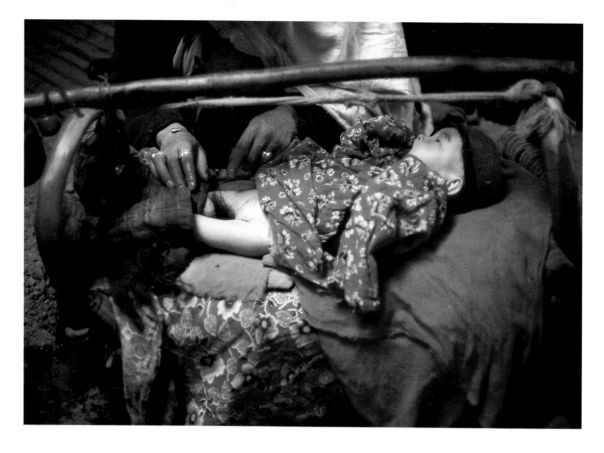

Afghanistan.
Putting yak hair in
the diaper.

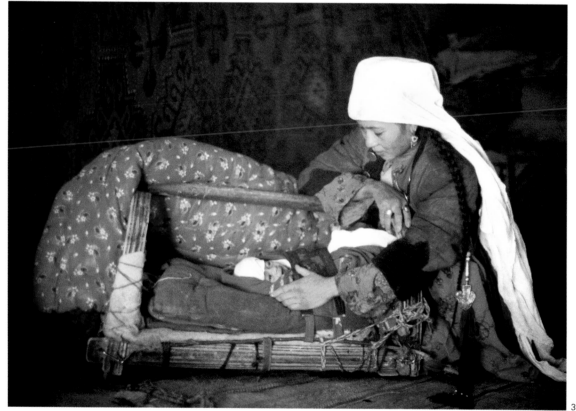

Cradling Legs

To rock her baby, an Afghan mother does not take him or her in her arms: she lays the baby along her legs with the little head resting on her feet, or a little cushion. She gently moves her legs to the right and the left until the child calms down and goes to sleep. She then puts the baby in the crib next to her own bed. For the first two years of life, the baby is never left alone at the mercy of evil spirits. The mother puts some earth into the little hand so that the child will sleep deeply. She puts a piece of bread or a prayer on the child's breast so that her baby will not be afraid.

Left and opposite:
Afghanistan.
Kirghiz cradles.

3

Qatar.
A Bedouin baby in
a cradle.

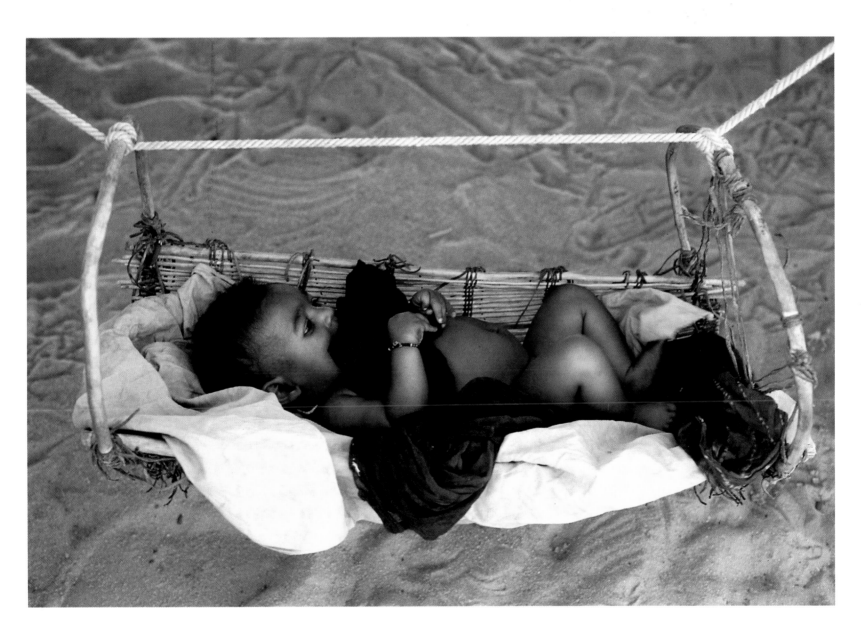

Mauritania.
A Tuareg baby in a
cradle that may be
hung on a camel.

The Message of Lullabies

"In a cradle of date wood, my treasure / In a cradle of bamboo, my treasure / Is my baby asleep? / In a cradle the shape of an elephant's head, my treasure / Is my baby wriggling?" Hélène Stork has watched how Indian mothers sing and chant the calming tunes of sweet lullabies—inspired by ancient Tamil literature or handed down from ancestors—to rock their children to sleep. The mother sings of the beauty of the gods and of her child, she makes vows for her baby, she praises the wisdom, riches, or courage of family members, and she interprets her baby's tears.

Cradle songs are often improvised, sometimes consisting of repetitions of sounds and words that seem devoid of sense, but which envelop the baby with their reassuring regularity. In Siberia, among the Inuit, songs of affection are invented spontaneously, and are sometimes reduced to little sounds, ono-matopoeia, or a phrase that is "unique, made just for this baby," says Bernadette Robbe. "He is round, he is shiny / Like a little bit of ice in the water / He hops / He floats / He plays / Like a little bit of ice in the water / Aya aya yek! / Raise your eyes / Look at me / Little bit of ice in the water."

In Africa, Pygmy fathers "yodel" lullabies to their babies. These songs, often taken up by the whole family, are long and loud and weave a sonorous cocoon around the child. But it is among the Chácobos in the Amazon Basin that the role of lullabies is perhaps the strangest. Fathers who want to become shamans often invent lullabies to protect their children, the *nahuariti*. Fathers rock in their hammocks with their baby in their arms, and talk about domestic spirits, exhorting the child not to be afraid. It is hard to tell if the songs are addressed to the spirits or the children: "Perhaps that's the key to everything," Philippe Erikson interprets, "If you treat the spirits as if they were your own children, you reduce the risks and may be able to control the situation."

Nigeria.
A mother and her
children in the Aïr.

The Song of Tears

All over the world, parents are patient and gentle in order to prevent their infant's tears, which can attract demons. African mothers imitate their baby's babbling, both to calm them and to cover up the sound of their voices. Consoling a baby always takes on a certain urgency. When a Chinese child cries at night, a magic spell is written on a piece of yellow paper. In order for it to take effect, it must be posted in the street, at midnight, without anyone seeing.

The parents also take preventive measures. Among the Kabyles, women pour water at a crossroads while walking backwards and speaking the ritual words: "these are the tears of my son (or my daughter) that I am stopping. I am not pouring out water." Jacques Lizot reports an extraordinary technique practiced in the Metidja called "calming with a knife." After birth, the grandmother puts the baby in a sieve placed on the ground. The knife that was used to cut the umbilical cord is driven into the earth in such a way that it touches the sieve. When the child cries, and the parents want to calm him or her, they vibrate the blade by pushing on the hilt. Among the Kabyles, the knife that was used to cut the umbilical cord, the water used for washing the baby, seven pieces of wood with wool wrapped around the ends, and some salt are put into a pot. As soon as the baby starts to cry, the parents shake the knife and sticks, and the noise scares away the evil spirits that are keeping the child from going to sleep.

For the Tuaregs of Niger, the newborn cries because the angels have just said, "You have come into the world and you will die." The parents know how much comforting the baby needs. But sometimes babies themselves manage to communicate why they are sad. In Bolivia, among the Chácobos, infants cry like all the other infants in the world, but they learn how to sob rhythmically before they learn to speak. "To my ears," says Philippe Erikson, "it sounds like music."

157

Afghanistan.
A baby from
Nuristan in a basket
cradle.

Cocoons and Carriers

According to their way of life—nomadic or sedentary—and the materials available—skin, wood, bark, bamboo, reed, cork, palm, wool, or cotton—parents make all different sorts of cradles ranging from the most humble—something improvised at a moment's notice to free the mother's arms for work, such as a piece of fabric tied to a tree branch—to the most finely crafted, such as Oriental cradles inlaid with pieces of mother-of-pearl. Among the Tuaregs of Hoggar, the baby may be laid in a cardboard box or an animal skin, the head wedged in place with old rags.

The structure and shape of a cradle varies depending on the society and the climate: hammocks of light fabric or little baskets of reeds hung up in an airy spot in the house; Siberian cradles that look like hanging tents; or, among the Lapps, wooden shells shaped like wooden shoes that contain the baby as if in a giant boot. In many regions of the world, where furniture is kept to a minimum, there are no closets, and personal possessions are often hung up. The baby is no exception, and in this way is kept away from the ground and from animals.

India.
A nomadic Marwari father with his children in Rajasthan.

Defensive Arsenal

Cradles are often equipped with bunches of amulets that serve both to distract the baby and chase off evil spirits. Shells, bells, coins, beads, and bone clappers are attached to the cradle or to the baby's hood, following the same principles as the "baby gates" found in the West. In Mongolia, mobiles made of fringe and little triangles of colored fabrics, the points of which are supposed to keep off the spirits, are hung above the baby.

In place of gifts such as the teddy bears found in Western cradles, people in Thailand choose objects that are designed to influence the child's destiny. A little boy whose parents want him to be a good worker receives a machete; if they want him to be intelligent, he receives a pen; a little girl often receives needles. Sweet-smelling plants or spices such as oleander, cumin, and benzoin may be put under the diapers. Sometimes the cradle itself is dyed and scented with turmeric or saffron. In this way, the noises, colors, movements, and smells that stimulate the newborn's senses form a protective screen against the supernatural creatures that lurk around the cradle.

The Kabyles set a system of traps, decoys, and defensive rituals around the baby. On the day when the mother goes to the fountain for the first time after giving birth, she carries some water back in her mouth, even though the spring may be a long way off. She then empties the water in her cheeks under the cradle so that her child will lie quietly, like sleeping water. The baby is rarely left alone, but if the mother must leave, she takes care to put a container of water under the cradle to keep the spirits—as if they were ants—from getting to the baby.

Tibet.

Drogpa nomads in Pekhutso, a region of the Himalayas.

Baby Nests

In general, babies are put to sleep on their backs. But often they are elevated by a little pillow or pile of cloths, or better yet, put in a half-sitting position—as in Siberia—from which they are able to watch the world around them at leisure. In Indonesia, babies must not sleep completely stretched out, since that is the posture of the dead (as in the past in Europe, when people slept in an almost sitting position against a pile of pillows). All who are sick or in a critical situation must avoid the prone position—young mothers spend forty days sitting after they give birth, and the sick must never stretch out. Very young babies are sometimes hung from the ceiling, almost vertically, like strange bundles of cloth. The cocoons in which these babies live and sleep are quite odd.

Jean-Claude Jugon writes that in Japan the newborn is put into a big basket, an *ejiko*, made of finely woven rice straw lined with ashes, straw, rice husks, seaweed, or charcoal. Carried everywhere in this nest, wrapped up in warm blankets, the baby leaves the *ejiko* only when it is time to learn to walk. According to popular belief, it is important never to leave the *ejiko* empty, for fear that a spirit of contradiction might come and take up residence.

Indonesia.
Dyak baby in a
cloth cradle hang-
ing from the roof
of a house in
Borneo.

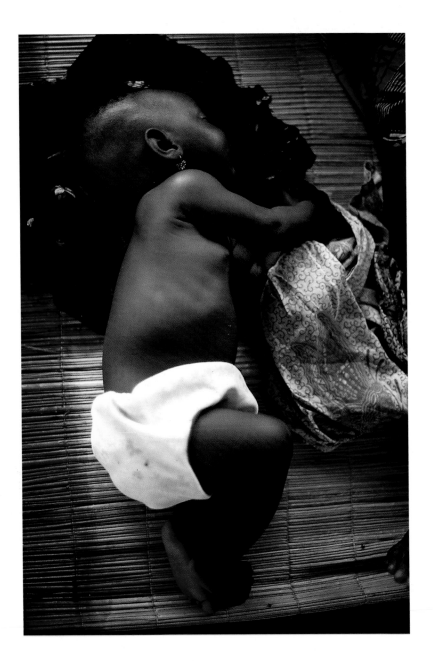

Benin.
Babies sleeping on
a mat and a
boubou.

The Rhythm of Rocking

The African baby sleeps lying on a mat, nestled against the mother, within reach of her breast. The mother calms her baby with rhythmical pats on the back or the chest. During the day she soothes her child with the rocking motion of her breasts, against which the baby is cuddled. Unique to Pygmy parents is the manner in which they rock their infant to sleep in their hands with an up and down movement. The rhythm of cradling is related to the mother's movements: the African baby sleeps surrounded by the noises of everyday life, and of songs, and is vigorously shaken or jiggled. This acoustic and tactile accompaniment is far removed from the conditions in which the Western baby, who "needs" silence and softness, falls asleep. In many other regions of the world, where cradles or hanging hammocks make rocking easier, the rocking is usually quite vigorous. Among fishing tribes in Malaysia, fathers rock their babies with the same force and in the same rhythm they use when rowing.

Rocking does not always have to do with sleep: many peoples rock their wide-awake babies during the day. In India, as soon as the baby begins to move or cry there is always someone at hand to push the little hammock to start it swinging. In the northwest of Brazil, parents rock their wide-awake babies while they play with or care for them. This rocking is supposed to calm them, and also to stimulate them—it keeps them in a "calm and attentive state of waking," as Gloria Meta explains. She points out that in this part of the world, "even adults rock themselves all their lives." However, she notes, "rocking movements follow a very individual rhythm related to the development of the child." In fact, a grave danger always hovers over the baby: the illness caused by being "startled," which may be provoked by any physical or auditory shock that is too violent.

Ivory Coast.

A baby lying in a plastic bathtub lined with cloths.

Little Litter

Nice and warm, Indian babies were wrapped up in little blankets of doe skin, rabbit skin, or reindeer hide. Different materials could be used for diapers, such as crumbled sage bark, dried moss, powdered bison dung, swamp rushes, and sweet-smelling grasses. The stuffing was changed when dirty.

The Hopi in Arizona diapered their baby with supple and absorbent cedar bark, which was rubbed with sand when wet and then dried in the sun. This method of diapering is found in many other places in the world. Among the Amdo of Tibet, the baby is put into a sack of animal skin, which is stuffed with the dung of cows, rams, and wild sheep—all these agile animals transfer their qualities to the child. The dried manure has lost its disagreeable smell.

Portable Cradles

"My little one! / My sweet one! / My little girl! / You're only a baby / But the time / To play with you, my baby / Will go by quickly / My little one! / My charming little bit of woman!"

Leaning against a tree trunk, or hanging from a branch in a papoose, the Sioux baby does not leave his or her mother, who takes the child and her little bed with her when she works. The Indians of North America lived in their cradles from birth until they started walking. These little pieces of furniture took the place of both beds and baby carriers. Wrapped in their blankets, securely tied with string, the little Indians became accustomed to, and even liked, their "nests." Caroline Nietammer relates that an Apache woman told her that after her son had started walking, he would carry his papoose around on his back if he was tired or sad.

China.
A cradle from the
Dafur region.

China.
A mother and her
baby in the Oroqen
region.

Wood, Leather, or Reed

Whether hollowed out of wood, made of boards, cut and sewn from skins attached to wooden laths, or woven with willow or reeds, the sturdy cradles of the American Indians protected their babies perfectly. Materials were carefully chosen; for example, the wood of Navajo cradles was chosen from the east side of an intact tree that had been protected from lightning, wind, or even bears' claws. Among these Indians, the cradle was a microcosm of the universe that incorporated the heavens and the earth. Bead decorations, fringes, colors, symbols, and designs ornamented the cradles, protected the child, and identified the tribe to which he or she belonged. Often made by the grandmother, the cradles were a part of the family heritage. Sometimes they were so identified with the child that if the child died, the cradle would be thrown away, burned, put on the child's grave, or buried with the child lying inside, just as he or she had while still alive.

Chapter Five

Pygmy Fathers, Peul Uncles, and Papuan Mothers

The Baby in the Family

The baby's great fragility has caused parents to imagine a whole world of shadow people always hungering for human infants. Sorcerers, spirits, and ogresses devour the babies, or their invisible doubles. The smell of babies and the noises they make delight the spirits. So parents have discovered all sorts of tricks, sometimes actual little plays, designed to ensnare these spirits. In Africa and Asia, parents pretend to sell their babies at the market as if they were commodities. If babies get sick, their names are changed in order to disguise this weakness—they are then called "It's not him," "Cannot be thrown out," or even "Garbage." Parents have developed an arsenal of potent decoys to trick the spirits: among the Kabyles, the mother takes the bone from a rotting carcass, covers it with honey, and wraps it in a baby blanket.

But evil spirits are not the only danger. As a creature wandering between two worlds, the baby has a vagabond soul, tenuously attached to the little body. At the least setback, the fugitive soul may escape. If babies' families do not pamper them enough, infants may prefer to return to their companions from the beyond. If the baby's life force seems to have left the child after a fright or an illness, the parents, as if looking for a little cat, try ritual calls for the baby's soul. Among the Muong in Vietnam, parents take a handful of rice, a cooked egg, a long spatula, and a ladle and stand by the front door crying, "You, the three souls and the seven life forces, male and female, wherever you may be, come back to your father and mother and eat well."

In China, the baby's spirit is called back while the child is sleeping. Little slippers are hidden under the baby's pillow, and at midnight, while caressing her infant, the mother whispers, "Little one, come back through the mountains, I'm calling you, you've answered, blessed be the ancestors of three generations and the god of the hearth who is in charge of life and death, the true inferior and superior souls of my baby have returned." Parents will do anything to hold onto their baby. Kabyle mothers go so far as to suckle bats, which are believed to cause diarrhea in infants, and while doing so they threaten, "I've given you my promise, you have had a drop of milk from me. If you betray me concerning my children, may God betray you!"

Central African Republic:

An Aka Pygmy mother and her baby.

169

Cooking the Placenta

In the West, the placenta is discreetly disposed of. It often provokes a certain revulsion. Elsewhere, families deal with it differently: it is washed, kneaded, put in a pot, buried, wrapped in leaves, hung in the trees, or eaten. Everywhere in the world, the treatment of the afterbirth includes many rites. George Condominas tells us that among the Muong in Vietnam, the young mothers who are present after a birth have their babies trample the blood that flows from the placenta so that, when they grow up, they will not fight with the newborn. Elsewhere in Vietnam, among the Muong, the placenta is enclosed in a joint of bamboo, then hung in the forest next to other bamboo tubes stuffed with placenta that have been brought there over the years by mothers.

The placenta is sometimes thought to be the baby's companion, or a twin, and is also often considered a very appetizing food. Among the Yakuts of Siberia, it is prepared as a dish, and baby's father feasts on it. Among the Inuit, the placenta is dried and saved, and the child eats a piece for his or her first food. A piece is eaten at each major childhood event, such as the first anorak or the first kayak.

The placenta may also serve as a sort of life-activation force: among the Kisii of Guinea, it is ground up with earth and put in a pot that is buried at the bottom of a hole in the courtyard behind the dwelling. If in the first few days the baby cries and does not develop well, the mother vigorously remixes this potion to give new force to her baby. One of the most moving ceremonies is reported by Claude Rivière: among the Ewe of Togo, the midwife effects a pact between the mother and the child. She puts a little bit of the cut-up cord on the mother's forehead and breast, then on the child's, while saying, "Child, if your mother calls, answer her. Mother, when you hear your child cry, hurry to see what's wrong."

Cameroon.
A young Pygmy woman lying on a carpet of leaves in the forest.

170

Sorcerer Babies

An unexpected, supernatural event takes place in a little village in Benin: two babies, not just one, see the light of day. Whether they are viewed as a blessing or a curse, twins provoke fear in the parents, and sometimes the whole village. The birth of twins always provokes ambivalent feelings. Depending on the region of the world, these exceptional beings, endowed with magical powers, are accepted only with a great many precautions, and are sometimes simply rejected. A menace to their parents' lives, the fruit of an adulterous relationship with a neighbor or a spirit, guilty of incest in the belly of their mother (if they are of different sexes), twins are often put to death. Sometimes only one of them is killed: both cannot survive, since they share a soul.

But even in regions where twins are considered a sign of fertility, bringing good luck and honor for those close to them, fear persists. To neutralize the apprehension caused by the birth of twins, and to channel the dangers inherent in these visionary beings, soothsayers, who are intimate with the invisible, perform specific rituals associated with the prohibitions and prescriptions regarding the care given to these children. In day-to-day life, the mother must treat both children with perfect equality: they must be fed, clothed, cared for, and soothed in exactly the same manner so as not to awake in them the pangs of a deadly jealousy.

Contrary to the beliefs of Western psychology, in some countries in the world, twins are thought to be one and the same person. In Africa, they are viewed as existing halfway between the human and the divine, and are honored from birth like kings or chiefs.

Below and opposite: Benin. A celebration of the cult of twins in the voodoo religion.

The Geography of Kisses

In Africa, the mother's bosom, which provides nourishment, also provides the best way to comfort or cuddle the baby—the breast plays the role of nipple, toy, or pacifier. Nestled against her, the African baby is one with the mother's body. Loving looks and kisses do not seem as necessary as in the West, where the baby is often separated from the mother during the day. The fear of arousing the jealousy of evil spirits imposes a certain restraint on the mother's public displays of affection. Instead, the mother expresses her affection by anticipating the child's every desire. Day and night, careful attention is paid to the baby, whose continued existence is so uncertain, and who—if unhappy on earth—may still decide to return to the hereafter. This indulgence of the infant is not limited to Africa; it is almost universal. No restraints are placed on newborns, whose every wish is granted.

Babies are kissed by their mother, father, brothers, sisters, and by the people of the village. In Africa; the little one is often kissed on or in the mouth—which is not done between adults—and is calmed by tickles, nibbles, and pats. Among the Inuit, babies are cajoled, smelled, and inhaled, caressed and kissed on their sex organs, and rubbed on the nose. In Mongolia, the baby is sniffed rather than kissed. In the Amazon rainforest, Kayapo mothers squeeze their babies, caress their hair, and put their open mouths against their skin in a mute kiss. In New Guinea, the Baruya, like the Pygmies of Africa, do not kiss as adults—only the baby is covered with noisy kisses.

Cameroon.

A scene of everyday
life in a Fali village.

Tender Tidbits

Day and night, at any time, the baby is fed as soon as he or she seems hungry. But, often early on in the first year, sometimes as soon as the first week, the infant is given food other than breast milk. The baby is introduced to adult food slowly, in a psychological and symbolic progression from the soft to the hard, from the lean to the fat, from the mild to the strong. Boiled millet, sorghum, cassava, or gravy are first given to the child in minuscule quantities. Sometimes the mother dips her finger into the boiled meal to put it into her child's mouth. In Oceania, among the Arapesh, when the food is too runny to be fed to the child on a finger, it is soaked up in bark cloth, which is then given to the child to suck. But, most of the time, mothers use their mouths as a bottle, spoon, and mixer to administer solid food. They chew a mouthful before putting it between their child's lips. Through this mouth-to-mouth feeding, a mother transmits affection as well as prechewed food, "maternalized" by her saliva.

This manner of feeding, far from being an exclusively African practice, is found throughout the world. The Inuit mother, after chewing a little food and giving it to her baby, takes water in her mouth and quenches her child's thirst by slowly releasing it into the child's little mouth. In Oceania, the Yafars give their children fish, headless grubs, or liver in this way. Thus, by the time a baby is weaned, he or she already has a diversified diet. Everything is then used to discourage nursing: chili, pepper, and other spicy substances are spread on the mother's breast. Among the Yafars of Oceania, mothers rub their breasts with the skull of a dead person, which is kept in the house until that time.

Kenya.
Mouth-to-mouth
feeding among the
Maasai.

Ethiopia.
A Surma woman
and her baby. The
baby is playing with
a large disk of clay
inserted into the
mother's lower lip.

A Whispered Name

"Fat cheeks" for a chubby baby; "Bare bone" for a baby born without hair; "Feet first," "Brush," or "Market" according to the manner and place of birth; "No trouble" if the baby is born in the middle of family fights; "Mixed" if there is doubt about legitimacy; "Death's overdoing it" if the mother has lost several children—ethnologist Doris Bonnet reveals that the custom of using the name as a message is widespread in Africa. The name refers to the history of the family, and the circumstances in which the child was born. The baby also often bears the names of his or her ancestors; thus, it is necessary to decide which member of the family lives again in the child.

Until the baby is named, he or she is not a member of society and is not considered a full person; even the gender is indeterminate. The baby is sometimes given several names, or at least two: the real name, which must remain secret, and an everyday name. The mother, father, grandparents, or any other person authorized to give the child a name, whispers it in the baby's ear like a precious secret. The baby's name reflects the essence, or the very soul, of the infant and provides a hold for powerful evil forces. Its pronunciation must be avoided. The mother often calls the baby "the child," or "the little one," and the neighbors refer to the baby as "so-and-so's child." Names have so much power that they may even be designed to trick the spirits—people who have lost several children may call the next one "Garbage," "Pebbles," or "Footstool" in order to feign indifference toward the infant.

In Thailand, names are not given to children before a certain age in the hope that this anonymity will protect them from occult powers. In Oceania, children are not named until their survival is certain—they must be walking, and have their first teeth. In almost all societies, if a child gets sick it means that his or her name was poorly chosen, and the only treatment is "debaptizing."

Namibia.
A Himba mother with her baby in Kaokoland.

178

Spirit Traps

In Burkina Faso, a mother who has already lost several infants pretends to sell the newborn at the market in a basket in order to trick the spirits. Mossi parents always feign indifference or even contempt toward their newborns, an act that is widespread in traditional societies. Parents and visitors must not compliment the baby, or they risk arousing the jealousy of evil spirits. Publicly, the baby is often ignored. Among some peoples, the Dogons for example, mothers ritually insult their infants, look at them with anger, and spit on the ground in disgust.

There are many other ways to trick the spirits and protect the child: among the Tuaregs, the newborn sleeps on the ground for the first days concealed under a cloth, next to a knife. The baby's waste is not thrown away, but rather hidden under the bed because, like everything that comes from the infant, it may provide a hold to wicked powers. The baby's

hair is purposely left uncut so that he or she resembles a hairy genie, thus tricking the evil spirits. When a baby trudges through the sand, the footsteps are wiped out. Sometimes a decoy is left in place of the baby. In Algeria, parents are terrified of the demons that devour children and try to snatch newborns. Parents put a big wild colocynth, a melon that is as round and pale as the baby's head, next to the baby so that it will be carried off instead of the child. Among the Kabyles, Rahmani Slimane relates that a mother who has lost many children will prepare a bone from a carcass, and coat it with honey on the night of birth. She swaddles it like a baby and puts it by her side, where her baby should be, and the real baby is entrusted to the midwife. For three days and three nights, the ogress comes and licks the bone. On the third day, the bone is thrown far from the dwelling, and the ogress follows it.

Uganda.
A woman and her
baby.

Burkina Faso.

A Mossi woman
and her baby.

This page and
opposite:
Gabon.
Carrying heavy bur-
dens using a fore-
head band.

Ghost Babies

In traditional societies, infant mortality is still very high. Mothers usually lose several of their children. Often the newborn that has just died does not receive a real funeral and is not buried with the adults. The parents bury the infant next to the placenta or under a heap of dung as a way of saying to the spirits, "How could you be interested in our children when you see that we do not pay any attention to them ourselves?"

According to Doris Bonnet, among the Mossi, when a woman regularly loses her children at a young age, she believes that it is the same baby returning time after time. Before the burial, the parents mark the body with an incision on the ear or chest, or cut off a bit of the infant's finger. If the next baby is born with the same mark, it proves that it is the same baby. Sometimes multiple deaths are interpreted as being the work of an ancestor who comes to flatter women by giving them the illusion that they are mothers. Often babies fall sick and die because their life force has been devoured by a sorcerer, or because they were badly named, or because their birth catalyzed the family's past conflicts.

In China, it is thought that the dead child is a ghost creditor. Since the parents did not pay their debts in a previous lifetime, the ghost creditor lives in the child's body until the parents give him the sum owed. For these reasons, old women always forbid mourning a dead child. Sometimes the body is even mistreated—the parents may stab it—so that the spirit will not dare to come back. All these complex constructions exist as a way for people to make sense of the high infant mortality rate. According to some psychiatrists, these beliefs regarding ghost children promote an anesthesia among the bereaved that allows the mother to detach herself from her lost child and transfer her hopes on the newborn to come.

Brothers and Sisters

In the West, older children used to be relegated to the role of nanny; in traditional societies today, babies are often entrusted to their older sisters—who are often not much older. The famous ethnologist Margaret Mead criticizes this state of affairs, not without a certain humor, when she explains that in Samoa, for example, "The trusted nanny is a little six-year-old girl who carries the baby astride her hip or at her waist. These young nannies never encourage the children to walk: they know very well that a child who knows how to walk gets into more mischief." If Samoa were a country of small families, half its population would be subject to the tyranny and selfishness of the slightly older half. But, usually, just at the moment when the small child becomes unbearable for the older one, someone puts an even smaller one in his or her arms.

Watching babies is not merely a simple chore: in these societies without schools, the function of the babysitter is to provide an apprenticeship to the younger child in all areas, depending on the child's rank in society and the child's gender. What is more, the mother has no choice but to delegate some tasks. From the age of four or five years on, children are charged with watching the littler ones. But the weight of this responsibility is not as heavy as we would imagine. Watching little children is usually a collective task—the children belong to everyone and everyone watches over them, picking up and comforting any baby who comes within reach.

This page and opposite: Guinea-Bissau. Big sisters carrying their younger siblings in the Bijagos Islands.

Zaire.
A Pygmy sister and
brother.

Forbidden Animals

When a baby falls ill, there is a whole pharmacopoeia and a wide variety of rituals corresponding to each pathology. Ethnologist Alain Epelboin has filmed some of the treatments used among the Pygmies. If an infant is seized with convulsions, the healer slaps the baby with fresh leaves, then grinds the leaves together between his hands, extracting the juice, which he trickles into the baby's mouth and nostrils. He then energetically rubs the baby all over and holds the baby over the smoke of burning leaves. During this smoking, the mother utters spells and passes her breasts over the smoke, squirting a little milk on the coals before nursing her baby. Another remedy is to spread the charred bones and tail of a wild animal over the baby's body, even inside the nostrils.

In Africa, as in many regions of the world, there is a complex system of food taboos that vary widely depending on the tribe: if the parents eat a forbidden animal, their child will get sick. The Pygmy father and mother influence the health of their children by what they eat. Serge Bahuchet explains that forbidden animals are those that are not a part of everyday food, but are rare. Every society has its own perception of the world and tries to legislate the world in its own way—usually, forbidden animals are those that do not seem to have a natural place within the classification of animals; for example, the flying squirrel, which is somewhere between a bird and a mammal. Animals that have spots are also dangerous because they are related to the supernatural world. In Africa, the supernatural world has its own special color, usually white. Thus, animals with white spots are considered too powerful, too close to the spirits.

Elsewhere, food restrictions may include plants. In the Amazon, Kayapo parents-to-be cannot eat bananas, which soften the baby's head, nor yams or fibrous tubers, which make the baby too hairy. After birth, in order to protect the baby's fragile life, the parents are forbidden to make, eat, hunt, or fish for certain foods. If an infant falls ill, or dies, it is because the parents, or even the ancestors, have not respected these taboos: the soothsayer often discovers a violation that was committed two or three generations back.

Central African Republic.
Bayaka Pygmy women and children in front of their hut, sorting and peeling fruit they have gathered.

Pygmy Fathers

Bambiti, a two-month-old little girl, is seated on the lap of her father, Kakao, outside the hut. Kakao pours a little water into his hand, tips the baby's head back, and gives her a drink. He sits her on his knees, blows gently, and kisses her neck. It is now time for him to leave on a hunt with his net, so Kakao slips Bambiti into the baby carrier, takes his spear, and goes into the forest. His wife Tengbe follows behind carrying a basket. Kakao pauses to clean the baby's nose, then continues walking, singing to his baby. Fifteen minutes later, the baby is asleep in her father's arms.

Barry Hewlett has described in great detail numerous Aka Pygmy fathers with their children. While Aka mothers are always there for their babies, the fathers are also very attentive. They often carry the children, especially during the first months of life, and make sure they are not bitten by insects or snakes, or eaten by a panther. In the evening, fathers spend a good deal of time playing with their children in front of the hut. They hold the babies in their arms, awake or asleep, and wipe them with leaves when they do their business. At night, the children wake up often and it is common to see fathers humming or singing to calm them. If the child is particularly upset, it is more often the father who takes the baby outside to walk or dance with him or her. During the day, when the mother is cooking, or busy looking for wood, the father watches the children. According to Barry Hewlett, Aka fathers contribute more to child rearing than fathers in any other traditional society.

This page and opposite: Central African Republic.
Pygmy fathers with their children.

The Baby, the Stranger

Unlike Western parents, who consider their babies to be completely their own, parents in many ethnic groups think of babies as temporary guests whom it is important to treat well. Children to be born are none other than deceased relatives, or, more precisely, a component of the relative who has returned to the living. While waiting to come back to this world, African babies stagnate in a shadow world, which is most often aquatic. "It is from there, attracted by the noise, the laughter, and the lively humor of the women or children," explains Odile Journet, "that babies come to wander through the village, in search of a hospitable womb." During childbirth, a fire is constantly maintained to light the baby's path.

In Africa, newborns, by reason of their light skin color, are classified in the category of "white" beings, the color of the world of the dead, of ancestors, ghosts, and Westerners, who have assimilated with the creatures of another world. Among the Mossi of Burkina Faso, the baby is called "the stranger." Often the earthly parents are not considered the child's only progenitors. For the Mossi, procreation is the result of a spirit penetrating a woman's belly while she is having sexual relations. These spirits are small invisible beings, as numerous as the stars, with big heads. Whether the spirits are good or evil, they live in proximity to human beings at all times. Every woman has a store of children—her most delicate task is to convince them to come and share her world. In this belief system, the death of a child may be interpreted as a reclaiming of the child by the mother in the other world. In short, what is a baby? It is a container of life energy, the heir to a tradition, a composite of his or her ancestors, a sort of hybrid being, half-human and half-divine, which finally decides to remain on the earth.

Cameroon.

A father with his
two wives and their
two children in the
Maba region.

New Guinea.
A Yafar father "clothed" in his penis case.

New Guinea.
A Huli mother with
her children in the
southern highlands.

Taboo Babies

In New Guinea, Yafar families live in
stilt houses with the floor about three
feet above ground. Below is an empty
space into which the garbage falls
through a
little door. It is here, ethnologist Bernard
Juillerat reports, that the mother must go
to give birth, and must stay during the
period of confinement. She cannot stand
up straight here, and her family just
above her head can only talk to her, or
pass her food, through the cracks in the
floor. No men are allowed to enter this
crawl space. After the birth of his child,
the father does not speak of the event,
does not pay any attention to it, but
simply goes about his usual business.
Everything about birth is taboo—it is a
mystery of the realm of nature, of the
wild animal kingdom. The father does
not touch the baby or hold the child in
his arms until three or four months later.
Until then he ignores the baby from fear
of being contaminated by the blood of
the umbilical cord. The father must keep
away from the feminine impurities that
could make him vulnerable to spirits.
Only later will the father pay attention to
his baby, participate in his child's education, babysit while the mother is work-
ing, and give dietary advice.

This separation of father and baby is
not found everywhere in Oceania.
Margaret Mead reports that among the
Arapesh, the father helps his wife care
for the baby as soon as she returns
home. He brings water in coconut shells
to bathe the newborn, and gathers
leaves with a bitter smell that are supposed to drive off evil forces. He takes
care of cleaning the baby, and feeds the
child soup from a coconut-shell spoon,
demonstrating as much patience as the
mother. The day upon which the baby
smiles at the father for the first time is
the day the child receives a name.

Invisible Newborns

In the Amazon rainforest in Brazil, the Matis women of the village assemble to welcome the newborn. Ethnologist Philippe Erikson notes that as soon as the baby arrives, one of the women or godmothers—not the mother of the child—takes the baby in her arms. The newborn is a spirit of the forest and not yet a human being. Still invisible, the child must go through a number of ritual steps—in particular giving back his or her first ornaments a few hours after birth—before becoming a person. Once the infant has been washed by the god-mothers, the baby receives anklets, bracelets, and, most important, a neck-lace made of monkey teeth. If the birth is sudden and unexpected, or happens at night, everyone panics. It is absolutely imperative to find animal teeth—mar-moset or monkey teeth are the most highly prized, but teeth of lower quality will suffice if these cannot be found.

The baby's ornaments are purposely made very crudely. They mark the baby's attachment to the women, and make the little being visible, but only to the female sex. Men, in particular the father, can still not look at the baby—the father's gaze is too strong, and his power must be controlled or it will be harmful for the baby. For the same reason, fathers cannot yet take their babies in their arms. This fear of a paternal over-dose goes away only after several months, when the baby's harness is put away. This ceremony, which marks a kind of rebirth for the child, brings to-gether all the women of the village. The harness, a substitute for the umbilical cord, is a collar crossing the torso made of beads carved from the shell of a palm fruit. It replaces the umbilical cord, which is hung from the mother's ham-mock after the birth. When it dries up and drops off, the mother hangs it from a palm tree, whose fruit is used to make the beads of the harness. Thanks to these "jewels," the baby finally becomes "visi-ble" to men. The father may now look at the baby and take him or her into his arms, but only in moderation.

Above and opposite: Brazil.
Matis mothers, a father, and children in the Amazon rain-forest.

Guyana.

A Camopi mother
cutting up an iguana.

India.
A Gallong father
sharpening his
knives with his
baby on his back.

Couvade

In many societies, the father must rest quietly and not bear arms after the birth of his child. This ritual, called couvade, is often very strict. For three days, the Wayapi father must not get out of his hammock or leave the family dwelling, except for a few furtive minutes at night. By observing a strict fast in absolute solitude, he scrupulously follows the ritual of paternal couvade, quite widespread in the Amazon Basin. Françoise Grenand explains that among the Wayapi, couvade has two objectives: to transfer onto the father the ill will of the evil spirits that threaten the fragile newborn, and to concentrate all the father's energy so that he may transfer it to the body and soul of the child, strengthening him or her.

During these days of isolation, the father is in communion with his child. His spirit remains near the infant, so it is easy for him to transfer a part of himself. The new soul that is created is fractious and disobedient, so the father must use his composure to tame the infant and teach him or her good manners. "The father and his newborn child are one and the same person: the child's soul is intimately linked with the soul of the father and everything that happens to the father during these critical days is supposed to affect the tender child immediately," writes Lucien Lévy-Brühl.

Even in societies where a new father is allowed to indulge in some activity, he must, nonetheless, concern himself at all times with his child, who is supposed to accompany him everywhere—even if the child is sleeping quietly next to the mother. For example, if the father climbs a tree, he must attach little sticks to the trunk to help the child's spirit climb up behind him; if he crosses a stream, he must leave a calabash floating in the water to help the spirit cross this obstacle.

Nigeria.
A Wodaabe uncle
and child.

Baby in Quarantine

While in the West, the newborn is associated with the idea of absolute innocence and purity, almost everywhere else in the world the newborn and mother are considered to be impure, polluted beings who must be segregated. Confined to a room, hut, or yurt sometimes specially built for this purpose, the mother eats from dishes that are kept for her use alone and that will soon be discarded. The blood of childbirth is an archetypal dangerous substance. In China, the mother and baby, called respectively "bloody being" and "bloody child," are forbidden to leave their room for a month, and are especially forbidden to appear in broad daylight.

But quarantining the baby is also a way to protect him or her. At this young age, the child is too feeble to be walked in the village anyway; but, more important, there is intense supernatural activity around the woman who has just given birth. Babies are real delicacies for evil spirits. Among the Tuaregs, the woman remains cloistered for seven days in her wooden bed, her back turned to the north, where the spirits live, her baby nestled to her belly. In China, after birth, the room's windows are quickly closed off with paper and the ventilation hole in the roof is blocked with bits of netting so that evil spirits cannot get into the baby's room. There is another reason for confinement: according to Jean-Paul Eschilmann, the quarantine room is a "death to the beyond," a tomb that is situated between two lives. The baby is a person who has died elsewhere and is born here.

Niger.
A Tuareg camp at dawn in the Aïr.

The First Outing

When the confinement is over, it is time to take the baby outside to present him or her to the clan or the village. This first walk is also a solemn way of giving the future landlord a tour of his house, his domain. Among the Muong in Vietnam, the baby crosses the threshold of the house in order to be presented to the sun. The father displays everything the baby will one day inherit: a hoe, a calabash, a pipe, a turban, a saber, and a crossbow. He shows them one by one to the child and explains their uses. Then the newborn pays a visit to all the neighbors. In each home, the mistress of the house anoints the baby with a magic plant in recognition of his or her entrance into the village community.

These ritual walks take place at various ages. In the Metidja in Algeria, at the time of the child's first haircut (around ten months of age), the paternal grandmother puts her grandchild on her back and, accompanied by several little girls in flamboyant costumes, they go from house to house, singing. The neighbors give grains of barley or wheat, or eggs, and sometimes money.

Kabyle mothers take their babies outside in the morning, at the time the shepherds lead their flocks to the fields. Various items, such as a pistol, a dagger, a sickle, and a billhook, are hung from the baby's swaddling clothes so that he or she will be brave and a good worker.

Rahmani Slimane reports a very curious ritual: upon returning from the fields, the mother sits on the doorstep and unknots her hair, dividing it in two and crossing the two strands on the chest of the child seated on her knees. She wraps her hair around the baby's toes and presses her breasts against the baby's hair to moisten it with her milk. During this time, the midwife pretends to take thorns from the baby's feet with a needle. She repeats three times, "I take the thorns from your path." There are other places in the world where the rituals surrounding the baby's first outing are much more simple: among the Arapesh of New Guinea, the baby is taken outside when he or she smiles for the first time.

Saudi Arabia.
A Bedouin mother
and her child.

The Dust of the Koran

In Muslim countries, as in most countries, babies are suckled as soon as they cry—the Koran even declares that suckling is a "right" of the child up to the age of two years. The mother must take care not to let a single drop of milk fall on the child's sexual organs, for fear that it will cause impotence or sterility. The newborn is not fed at all for the first few days, because colostrum—the fluid produced by the breasts before the milk—is considered evil. Nonetheless, the baby receives a first food that is highly symbolic.

In Afghanistan, right after birth, the Koran that sits on the shelf is dusted off and put into the baby's mouth. Among the Tuaregs of Niger, a similar ritual takes place on the day following birth. According to Saskia Walentowitz, a learned man chews a date, then pours some water over a little wooden board upon which are written verses from the Koran. This water is mixed with the chewed date and put into the baby's mouth. The baby must then be fed with real milk before this taste fades, so that he or she will always have a healthy appetite. A woman of exceptional moral character is chosen for this first nursing. This choice is important, since the milk is believed to go right into the baby's skull, transmitting the character traits of the nurse. A single feeding is enough to create a family relationship. When a woman becomes pregnant again, she immediately ceases to nurse, since her milk then becomes a poison. This weaning is sometimes very sudden. Sylvie Heslot tells how in Afghanistan, the mother rubs her nipples with a bitter plant, or sometimes even wool or hair.

Afghanistan.
A woman nursing her baby under her chador.

Afghanistan.

A Turkmen mother
and her baby.

Boy or Girl

In the countries of the Maghreb, the coming of a male baby is loudly announced—the men fire their rifles and the women ululate. Among the Pashtuns of Afghanistan, the celebrations also depend on the sex of the child. For a girl, the giving of a name is enough; for a boy, the festivities are more lavish. In China, the midwife cries "Great joy!" if the baby is male, but she is silent if it is a girl. Sometimes the baby girl is even named "Change" in the hope that the next baby will be a boy. Among the Inuit, the midwife pulls on the penis of the baby so that it will not be absorbed into the body, and the baby will not turn into a girl. Among the Ladakhi of Kashmir, the parents go so far as to hide the birth of a boy and pretend that he is a girl, in order to ward off the evil spirits and avoid the neighbors' jealousy.

As they grow up, children continue to be treated differently according to their gender. Among the Tuaregs of Hoggar, boys are weaned six months later than girls because they are thought to be more fragile. In other regions, nursing is prolonged in hopes of making boys stronger. Often male babies are massaged more energetically to make them more solid and tougher than girls.

But all these rituals and techniques should not make us think that parents love their male children more: they are designed, above all, to prepare the child for his or her future status and role. A Mossi mother shows her attachment to her little girl during the baby's first massage. She puts pressure on the little girl's breasts so that they will not grow too fast—meaning she could keep her daughter with her that much longer.

Creatures between Two Worlds

When babies gurgle or cry in their sleep, they are communicating with the spirits. Whether asleep or awake, little children in many parts of the globe associate with the supernatural world. In Mongolia, from the time of birth until the first haircut, the child is thought of as an intermediary being, a part of the family but not yet a part of society. To become a part of the latter, babies must first break their bonds with the invisible universe that is peopled with spirits.

In Africa as well, babies are not completely anchored to earthly life. They have special affinities with water spirits, and also spirits of the brush or the steppes, with whom they chatter and play—and who frighten them. Depending on the country, the period during which the baby is a messenger between two worlds may last until the first haircut, the first tooth, or until the child is weaned or has learned the language—as soon as the baby learns to speak the language of humans, he or she loses the ability to communicate with spirits. Doris Bonnet reports that among the Mossi of Burkina Faso, people say that "those behind them have closed their mouths," meaning that the spirits will not let babies give away their secrets.

India.
A Tibetan mother
and her baby in
Ladakh.

Children Sent Back

"The Dyaks who abandon children in trees and the Mongols and Algonquins who leave them on the edges of paths think that babies are easily reincarnated. This is not infanticide, but a return to the kingdom of death and rebirth. The death of a child is not a real death: children are not yet completely separated from the spirit world and they can return there easily," writes Edgar Morin. However, many peoples do not hesitate to do away with some newborns. Exposed in the depths of the bush, or left naked on an ice floe, infants are killed for two main reasons: malformed newborns are considered to be changelings left by sorcerers who have carried off the real child and left a monstrous creature in its place, which should be killed and sent back from whence it came; the other reason is the practical concern of being unable to ensure the child's survival because of famine, or because of the long trips taken by nomadic peoples. The child may also be entrusted to, or adopted by, someone else. The baby is no one's property, not even the parents'.

In Africa, the baby is a "piece of the group." Thus, babies have many possible mothers: it is common that an infertile woman will be entrusted with, or "loaned" a child of a very fertile woman. It gives her great joy to be seen at the market with a baby on her back. A woman who has lost all her children at an early age can symbolically "give away" her last-born in order to escape this fate. Most of the time, adopted children know their biological parents, whom they continue to see. Everyone feels like the parents of all the children, and the latter benefit from having many mothers.

Nepal.
A little Newar girl with her younger brother, made up and coated with mustard oil in Bhaktapur.

A Slow Birth

In India, among the numerous ceremonies to welcome babies, such as ear-piercing rituals, shaving the head, and celebrating the tenth day, the feast during which the name is given is one of the most important. Once named, the child is final-ly integrated into the community in which he or she will live. Biological birth does not coincide with social birth—the passage from one world to the other progresses by a series of steps that serve to create the person, as if the newborn must diversify little by little, gathering the material necessary to become completely human.

These successive births take the form of rituals that often accompany the key stages of development, such as eating solid food, teething, walking, and being weaned. These ceremonies organized by the community humanize the baby and incorporate him or her into society. Do-minique Champault relates how after a birth in the Algerian-Moroccan Sahara, the midwife whispers a litany into the newborn's ear: "The master engendered the heavens, the day with its sun, the night with its stars, the moon, the rain, and the clouds." This poetic list endures as the inspiration of an old woman. It is important not to forget anything, since forgetting a phenomenon or an animal can ultimately prove dangerous for the child.

Jean-Michel Mignot describes a ritual performed by the Koma in Cameroon: when a baby is born, the grandfather quickly and discreetly makes a minia-ture bow with which he very carefully shoots a tiny arrow at the newborn while softly reciting a little prayer to welcome the child. Among the Hopi in northern Arizona, during the celebration of walk-ing, the child is given a new name and new moccasins with a little hole in the sole of each—this way, if it happens that the baby is called back to the other world, he or she can answer that it's impossible to travel with worn-out moccasins.

India.

A naming ceremony in Shahdapur.

Teasing Kinship

In Asia, as in Africa, relationships between father and son are highly structured and relatively strict, while surprisingly equal relationships spring up between grandparents and grandchildren. People in Africa even speak of "teasing grandparents." Often these teasing relationships may have sexual or matrimonial themes. A grandmother will call her grandchild "my little husband," and the child will answer, "my old woman, my old wife." They pretend to be of the same generation. They may even go so far as to indulge in a game of insults, but no one takes offense.

How are we to interpret this whimsical and subtle relationship between elders and their young relatives? "It is necessary," Suzanne Lallemand states, "to have regulatory mechanisms so that the family will function. But it would be unbearable if there were only a hierarchy. These societies add a measure of equality to the hierarchy . . . but not necessarily where we would add it."

In the West, brothers and sisters are considered equals, while in Africa a strict hierarchy exists between elder and younger siblings. Joking relations between grandchildren and grandparents constitute a sort of social safety valve. Grandmothers are highly sought after to watch the little ones—they often act as midwives, clean and massage the babies, comfort them during weaning, and take care of them while their mothers work in the fields—and the grandfathers gladly play with them. Among the Hausa, in Nigeria, the elder happily plays with his grandchild: "Hello, rascal! What a rascal you are!" he laughs, while the baby gazes at him in astonishment.

South Africa.
A Ndebele grandmother and her grandchild.

We would like to thank the team of ethnologists without whom this book would not have been possible. After spending years in the field, they were willing to grant us long interviews in order to share the fruits of their research.

Catherine Aballea discovered Mongolia in 1989. She has since returned six times—once for an entire year—to study the language and the local folklore, as well as birth and childhood rituals. She is writing her doctoral thesis on representations of the child and concepts of identity in Mongolia. She is the author of the following works: "Le Soleil et la lune dans les mythes mongols," *Les Mystères de l'aube: Scythe et slaves, Mongols, Arméniens, SLOVO*, vol. 14, Paris, INALCO, 1994, pp. 35–75; *Fixer la vie ou Grossesse et petite enfance en Mongolie*, DEA report, INALCO, 1994; co-authored with C. Suxbaatar, *Histoire de l'enfant au Yack noir*, Clichy, INALCO, 1991; co-authored with C. Suxbaatar, *Contes mongols*, Clichy, INALCO, 1990.

Solenn Bardet is a geographer. She spent a year and a half among the Himba shepherds in Namibian Kaokoland, and wrote her doctoral thesis on the consequences of damming the Eperba River (which threatens to flood the region) for the Himba. She is the author of *Pieds nus sur la mer Rouge*, Paris, Editions Robert Laffont, 1998.

Doris Bonnet, an ethnologist specializing in Africa, was a student of Denise Paulme and Marc Augé at the Ecole des Hautes Etudes en Sciences Sociales. She has spent many years researching the anthropology of illness in early childhood among the Mossi in Burkina Faso, and recently conducted studies on sickle-cell anemia in the Ivory Coast and in France. She is the author of many works, including *Corps biologique, corps sociale: La Procréation et l'interprétation de la maladie de l'enfant chez les Moosé du Burkina* [Faso], Paris, ORSTOM, 1998, and "L'Eternal Retour ou le destin singulier de l'enfant," *l'Homme*, vol. XXXIV, no. 3: 1994, pp. 93–110.

Blandine Bril is an adjunct professor at the Ecole des Hautes Etudes en Sciences Sociales, where she is in charge of the research group on "learning and context." She is the co-author, with H. Lehalla, of *Le Développement psychologique est-il universel? Approches interculturelles*, Paris, PUF, 1988; and the co-author, with P. Dasen, C. Sabatier, and B. Krewer, of *Ethnothéories parentales et représentations de l'enfant et de l'adolescent: une perspective culturelle comparative*, 1998, to be published by L'Harmattan. She directed the video *Le Portage au dos, quelles réalités?*, CEPCL-PRI ACC/EHESS, 1992, and co-directed, with J. S. Jo, A. Lammel, C. Occampo, and M. Zack, *Le Bain, de l'hygiène au jeu. Enfants de six cultures*, CEPCL-PRI ACC/EHESS, 1992.

P. ALIX

Alain Epelboin is a medical doctor, ethnologist, researcher at the CNRS, and a member of the Laboratoire de langues et civilisations à traditions orale (LACITO, CNRS), and of the URA 882. He conducts research into body work, and into the anthropology of sickness and healing. He has conducted anthropological fieldwork in eastern Senegal, in the urban area of Dakar; in the Central African Republic (among pygmy patients and healers); and in the Paris area (among children of African immigrants with lead poisoning and African AIDS patients). Among the works he has published are *Encyclopédie des Pygmées akas, techniques, langage et société des chasseurs cueilleurs de la forêt centrafricaine*, co-authored with J. M. C. Thomas and S. Bahuchet, Paris, Selat-Peeters (2 vols.), 1994–97, and *Chroniques du saturnisme infantile, enquête ethnologique auprès de familles parisiennes originaire du Sénégal et du Mali*, co-authored with N. Rez Kallah (1989–94), L'Harmattan, 1997. Among his works on videotape are, notably, *Chroniques pygmées en République Centrafricaine: "berceuse" aka*, CNRS audiovisuel, 1987; *La Fumigation de Boyangi*, Central African Republic, 1988; *Du savon dans les yeux, toilette d'une fillette peul bandée au sein* (Ibel, eastern Senegal), CNRS audiovisuel, 1991; and *Mort et naissance de Masiki*, CNRS audiovisuel, 1997.

Philippe Erikson has a Ph.D. in ethnology and is an adjunct professor at l'université de Paris X-Nanterre. He is a member of the Laboratoire d'ethnologie et de sociologie comparative of Nanterre. He has worked in three locations: with the Matis in the Brazilian Amazon; the Chacobos in the Bolivian Amazon; and with steelworkers in France. He is the author of many articles and one book: *La Griffe des aïeux. Marquage du corps et démarquages ethniques chez les Matis d'Amazonie*, Paris, Editions Peeters, 1996.

Bernard Formoso was born in Athens in 1957. He is the chairman of the department of ethnology, ethnomusicology, and prehistory at l'université de Paris X-Nanterre. He has conducted research among the Thais, the Chinese of Thailand, and various peoples from the mountains of Thailand, Laos, and China. He is the author, most recently, of the following works: *Ban Amphawan et Ban Han, le devenir de deux villages rizicoles du Nord-Est thailandais*, Paris, éd. ERC/CNRS, 1997; "Bad Death and Malevolent Spirits among the T[h]ai Peoples," *Anthropos* 93, 1998, pp. 3–17; "La Jambe pour le cœur, les prestations matrimoniales chez les Teochius de Thaïlande," *L'Homme* no. 141, 1997, pp. 55–82; and "Hsiu-Kou-Ku: The Ritual of Refining of Restless Ghosts among the Chinese of Thailand," *Journal of the Royal Anthropological Institute* (Man), vol. 2, no. 2, 1996, pp. 217–34.

Sylvie Heslot-Saïfi is an ethnologist specializing in rural life in Afghanistan. She has visited that country many times over the last fifteen years with a variety of humanitarian missions. She speaks the language, Farsi, fluently. She has taught "The Civilization of Afghanistan" for ten years at the INALC, and is currently completing her doctoral thesis in Persian studies. She is the author of several works of research, and, most notably, the following publications: *Maîtrise d'ethnologie*, Paris VII: "Accoucheuses traditionnelles, accouchements et soins aux nouveau-nés en Afghanistan"; *DEA d'anthropologie* (EHESS): "La Symbolique du corps dans les expressions persanes d'Afghanistan"; "Donner la vie," *Les Nouvelles d'Afghanistan*, no. 63, 1994; and "Fais dodo," *Les Nouvelles d'Afghanistan*, no. 66, 1994.

Bernard Juillerat was born in Lausanne in 1937. After studying literature in that city and teaching for a year in Kinshasa, he wrote his doctoral thesis on ethnology at the Sorbonne (1969) on a society in northern Cameroon, then conducted research in Papua New Guinea. He is currently a director of research at the CNRS in Paris. He is the author of the following works: *Les Enfants du sang. Société, réproduction et imaginaire en Nouvelle-Guinée*, Paris, Maison des sciences de l'homme, 1986 (English translation: *Children of the Blood*, Oxford–New York, Berg Publishing, 1996); *Œdipe chasseur. Une mythologie du sujet en Nouvelle-Guinée*, Paris, PRF, 1991; and *L'Avènement du père. Rite, représentation, fantasme dans un culte mélanésien*, Paris, CNRS/MSH, 1995.

Suzanne Lallemand studies the history of child rearing in France, and has studied childhood among the Mossis and the Guoins-Tyermas in Burkina Faso, among the Kotokolis in Togo, and among the Bataks in Indonesia. She is an ethnologist and research director at the CNRS. She is the co-author of the following works: with G. Delaisi de Parseval, *L'Art d'accommoder les bébés*, Paris, Seuil, new edition by Odile Jacob, 1998; with M. Guidetti and M. F. Morel, *Enfance d'ailleurs, d'hier et d'aujourd'hui*, Paris, Armand Colin, 1997; and *La Circulation des enfants en société traditionnelle. Prêt, don, échange*, Paris, l'Harmattan, 1991.

Jean-Michel Mignot is a member of the research groups at the CNRS that study the anthropology and ecology of food distribution, and comparative sociology and ethnology. From 1991 to 1996 he led a scientific mission in northern Cameroon financed by the Ministry of Science and Space and the Thyssen Foundation. The data collected during this long experience were used as a basis for a *thèse du troisième cycle* entitled "Premiers éléments pour une étude ethnoécologique des enfants Masa Bugudum: acquisition des savoirs ethnobotaniques et ethnozoologiques."

Miya Awazu Pereira da Silva is an obstetrician/gynecologist, a graduate of the university of Sao Paolo, Brazil, and an anthropologist at l'université de Paris VII. As a member of the joint CNRS/MNHN/Collège de France team since 1984, she has studied the morphogenesis of the top of the skull during the middle ages. She has most recently published the following works: with A. Czorny, O. Cussenot, and A. Zouaoui, "Le nouveau-né au Moyen Age et les bases anthropologiques de la 'déformation toulousaine,'" *Actes des 7ᵉ Journées Anthropologiques "l'Enfant, son corps, son histoire,"* Editions APDCA, Valbonne, 1997, pp. 129–55; "Anthropologiques," at the Musée Tavet-Delacour at Pontoise; and with Commissioner B. Poirier, *Catalogue "Anthropologiques:" déformations crâniennes artificielles, histoire, recherches et hypothèses*, Pontoise, 1997.

Joëlle Robert-Lamblin, docteur d'Etat ès lettres, is currently a director of research at the CNRS and a member of the anthropology research team at the musée d'anthropologie de l'Homme. Her training in ethnology at the museum during the early sixties led her to pursue it as her vocation. Her interest in the peoples and cultures of the Arctic was born from her long collaboration with professeur Robert Gessain. Since 1967 she has paid many visits to the Far North including ten scientific missions to the east coast of Greenland, one to the west coast, a stay in the Aleutians, and four expeditions to northeast Siberia. She is the author of the following articles and books: "Esquimaux (Eskimo)," *Encyclopædia Universalis*, vol. 7, 1988, pp. 277–81; and with Paul-Emile Victor, *La Civilisation du phoque*, vol. 1, *Jeus, gestes et techniques des Eskimos d'Ammassalik*, A. Colin–R. Chabaud; vol. 2, *Légendes, rites et croyances des Eskimos d'Ammassalik*, R. Chabaud, 1989.

Hélène Elisabeth Stork is a professor of clinical and transcultural psychology at the Institut de psychologie of the université René-Descartes (Paris V). She has conducted comparative research on mothering techniques in different cultures, notably in southern India, where she completed many scientific missions. She is the author of several books on ethnopsychology and scientific articles, among them *Enfances indiennes: Etude de psychologie transculturelle et comparée du jeune enfant*, Le Centurion, 1993; *Les Rituels du coucher de l'enfant–Variations culturelles*, Editions Sociales Françaises, 1993; and "Garçons et filles, pères et mères, dans la berceuse populaire. Contribution à l'étude des phénomènes transitionnels," in *Garçons et filles, hommes et femmes. Aspects pluridisciplinaires de l'identité sexuée*, co-edited with P. G. Coslin and S. Lebovici, PUF, 1997. She has directed several films, among them *Pour endormir Lakshmi*, CNRS audiovisuel (south India, 1982); *Seliamedu–Petits soins aux bébés dans un village tamoul*, CNRS audiovisuel, 1982; *Techniques de maternage dans différents cultures*, 1988, CERIPE; and *Bercements et berceuses dans différents cultures*, 1989, CERIPE.

Saskia Walentovitz was born in Germany, but has lived in France for many years. An anthropologist specializing in Touareg studies, she has spent long months in the field conducting research on gender, ritual, and early childhood among the Imazwaghan of Azawagh (Niger). She wrote "De la graine à l'enfant nommé. Venir au monde chez les Touaregs Kel Eghlal," in *Touaregs et autres Sahariens entre plusieurs mondes. Définitions et autres redéfinitions de soi et les autres,* directed by H. Claudot–Hawad, *Cahiers de l'IREMAM*, no. 7–8, 1996.

Nadine Wanono, an ethnologist, filmmaker, and researcher at the CNRS, has worked for some twenty years among the Dogon tribe. She is particularly interested in the social organization of women, and in this context has directed several films, among them *Ibani ou l'écharpe bleue*, CNRS audiovisuel, 1990; *Demain au bord de fleuve les cauris nous ramasserons*, 1987, CNRSAV-NFTS; *A l'ombre du soleil, funérailles et intronisation du Hogon d'Arou*, co-directed with P. Loudou, ARTE, 1997. She is also the author of *Ciné-rituel de femmes dogon*, Editions du CNRS, 1987, and *Les Dogons*, Editions du Chêne, 1996.

Bibliography

Badini, Amadé. *Naître et grandir chez les Moosé traditionnels*, drawing, ADDB, Paris: Ougadougou.

Beaudoin, Gérard. *Les Dogons du Mali*, Paris: Armand Colin, 1984.

Bonnet, Doris. *Corps biologique, corps social*, Paris: O.R.S.T.O.M., 1988.

Champault, Dominique. *Naissance à Tabelbala*, excerpt from the Journal of the Society of Africanists, volume 23, Paris: 1953.

Clastres, Pierre. *Chroniques des indiens Guayaki*, Paris; Human Ground, Plon, 1974.

Condominas, Georges. *Nous avons mangé la forêt de la Pierre-Génie Gôo, chronique d'un village Mnong Gar*, Paris: Mercury of France, 1957.

Cuisinier, Jeanne. *Les Mu'o'ng*, The Institute of Ethnology, 1948.

Desjeux, Catherine and Bernard. *Africaines*, Paris: L'Harmattan, 1983.

Dreyfus, Simone. *Kayapo du nord*, Mouton and Company: 1963.

Dupire, Marguerite. *Organisation sociale des Peul*, Paris: Plon, 1970.

Erickson, Philippe. *La Griffe des aïeux, marquage du corps et démarquages éthniques chez les Matis d'Amazonie*, Paris: Peeters Editions, 1996.

Erny, Pierre. *L'enfant dans la pensee traditionelle de l'Afrique noire*, Paris: L'Harmattan, 1990.

Erny, Pierre. *Les Premiers pas dans la vie d'un enfant d'Afrique noire, naissance et première enfance*, Paris: L'Harmattan, 1988.

Eschlimann, Jean-Paul. *Naître sur la terre africaine*, Ivory Coast: INADES edition, 1982.

F. Taylor, Colin. *Traditions indiennes, la vie quotidienne des indiens d'Amérique*, Paris: Nathan, 1997.

Germain, Georges-Hébert. *Inuit, peuples de froid*, Paris: Solar, 1996.

Godelier, Maurice. *La Production des Grands Hommes*, Paris: Fayard, 1982.

Grenand, Françoise. *La Longue attente ou la naissance à la vie dans une société Tupi, Wayapi du haut Oyapock*, French Guyana, Swiss Society of American Studies, bulletin no. 48, 1984.

Hermanns, Matthias. *Die Familie der Amdo-Tibeter*, K. Alber: 1959.

Heslot, Sylvie. *Accoucheuses traditionnelles, accouchements et soins aux nouveaux-nés en Afghanistan. Dissertation on Mastery*, University of Paris, 7.

Hewlett, Barry S. *Intimate fathers, the nature and context of Aka pygmy paternal infant care*, Ann Arbor: University of Michigan Press, 1994.

Juillerat, Bernard. *Œdipe chasseur, une mythologie du sujet en Nouvelle-Guinée*, Paris: PUF, 1991.

Kun, Yang. *La vie de l'enfant en Chine*, The A.M.I. Monthly Review: 1939.

Leininger, Madeleine. *Transcultural Nursing*, New York: John Wiley and Sons, 1978.

Leroi-Gourhan, Arlette and André. *Un Voyage chez les Aïnous, Hokkaido 1938*, Paris: Albin Michel, 1989.

Lestage, Françoise. *Le temps du mûrissement, anthropologie de la petite enfance à laraos, Peruvian Andes*, Thesis of the EHESS: 1992.

Lévy-Brühl, Lucien. *L'âme primitive*, Paris: PUF, 1927.

Lhote, Henri. *Les Touaregs du Hoggar*, Paris: Armand Colin, 1984.

Lizot, Jacques. *Le cercle des feux*, Seuil: 1976.

Lizot, Jacques. *Metidja, un village algérien de L'Ouarsenis*, Algiers: S.N.E.D., 1973.

Mead, Margaret. *Mœurs et sexualité en océanie*, Paris: Human Ground, Plon, 1963.

Morin, Edgar. *L'Homme et la mort*, Paris: Seuil, 1970.

Nietammer, Caroline. *Filles de la terre, vies et légendes des femmes indiennes*, Paris: Albin Michel, 1997.

Paulme, Denise. *Les gens du riz*, Paris: Plon, 1970.

Parker, Nertha. *Cody California Indian Cradle*, Los Angeles: Southwest Museum, 1940.

Ravololomanga, Bodo. *Etre femme et mère à Madagascar*, Paris: L'Harmattan, 1992.

Rivière, Claude. *Union et procréation en Afrique*, Paris: L'Harmattan, 1990.

Rongier, Marie-France. *Eveil à la vie centrafricaine*, Paris: Ministry of Social Affairs.

Saladin D'Anglure, Bernard. "Violence et enfantements inuit ou les nœuds de la vie dans le fil du temps," in *Anthropology and Society*, vol. 4, no. 2: 1980.

Smith, Mary. *Baba de Karo*, Paris: Human Ground, Plon, 1969.

Slimane, Rahmani. *Coutumes Kabayles du Cap Aokas*, Algiers: 1939.

Stork, Hélène. *Enfances indiennes, étude de psychologie transculturelle et comparée du jeune enfant*, Paris: 1986.

Stork, Hélène. *Les Rituels du coucher de l'enfant, variations culturelles*, under the direction of Hélène Stork, Paris: ESF, 1993.

Van Gennep, Arnold. *Les Rites de passage*, Paris: Picard, 1981.

Victor, Paul-Emile, Joelle Robert-Lamblin. *La Civilisation du phoque*, Paris: Armand Colin, 1989.

Whiting, Beatrice B. *Six Cultures, Studies of child rearing*, New York: John Wiley and Sons, 1963.

Zerdoumi, Nefissa. *Enfants d'hier, l'éducation de l'enfant en milieu traditionnel algérien*, Paris: Maspero, 1970.

Collective Works

Enfants et sociétiés d'Asie du sud est, under the direction of Jeanine Koubi and Josianne Massard Vincent, Paris: L'Harmattan, 1994.

Grossesse et petite enfance en Afrique noire et à Madagascar, collection connaissance des hommes, 1991.

Journal des Africanistes, vol. 51, booklet 1 and 2, 1981.

Mythes et Croyances du monde entier, vol. 4, Brépols.

Les Carnets de l'Enfance, no. 25, 1974.

Photograph Credits